Longman Study Texts

Absurd Person Singular

Longman Study Texts   General editor: Richard Adams

Novels and stories

Jane Austen
  Emma
  Pride and Prejudice
Charlotte Brontë
  Jane Eyre
Emily Brontë
  Wuthering Heights
Charles Dickens
  Great Expectations
  Oliver Twist
George Eliot
  The Mill on the Floss
  Silas Marner
Nadine Gordimer
  July's People
Thomas Hardy
  Far from the Madding Crowd
  The Mayor of Casterbridge
Aldous Huxley
  Brave New World
Robin Jenkins
  The Cone-Gatherers
D H Lawrence
  Sons and Lovers
Somerset Maugham
  Short Stories
John Mortimer
  Paradise Postponed
George Orwell
  Animal Farm
  Nineteen Eighty-Four
Alan Paton
  Cry, The Beloved Country
Paul Scott
  Staying On
Mark Twain
  The Adventures of Huckleberry Finn
H G Wells
  The History of Mr Polly
Virginia Woolf
  To the Lighthouse

Plays

Alan Ayckbourn
  Absurd Person Singular
  Sisterly Feelings
Oliver Goldsmith
  She Stoops to Conquer
Ben Jonson
  Volpone
Christopher Marlowe
  Doctor Faustus
J B Priestley
  An Inspector Calls
Terence Rattigan
  The Winslow Boy
Willy Russell
  Educating Rita
Peter Shaffer
  Amadeus
  Equus
  The Royal Hunt of the Sun
William Shakespeare
  Macbeth
  The Merchant of Venice
  Romeo and Juliet
Bernard Shaw
  Androcles and the Lion
  Arms and the Man
  Caesar and Cleopatra
  The Devil's Disciple
  Major Barbara
  Pygmalion
  Saint Joan
Richard Brinsley Sheridan
  The Rivals
  The School for Scandal
John Webster
  The Duchess of Malfi
  The White Devil
Oscar Wilde
  The Importance of Being Earnest

Editor: George MacBeth
  Poetry for Today
Editor: Michael Marland
  Short Stories for Today

Alan Ayckbourn

Absurd Person Singular

edited by
Richard Adams

with a personal essay by
Alan Ayckbourn

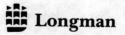 Longman

Longman Group UK Limited,
Longman House, Burnt Mill, Harlow,
Essex CM20 2JE, England
and Associated Companies throughout the world.

First published 1989

ISBN 0 582 01638 X

Set in 10 / 12 point Baskerville, Linotron 202
Produced by Longman Group (FE) Ltd
Printed in Hong Kong

Contents

Contents

A personal essay

by Alan Ayckbourn

The kingdom of the Hopcroft is at hand . . .

Absurd Person Singular was the fourth of my plays to be
performed in London's West End although, like its prede-
cessors, it started life in Scarborough in a modest 250-seat
theatre-in-the-round. The auditorium was a makeshift affair;
borrowed seats on rickety rostra in a small airless room of the
public library. On hot evenings, senior citizens would be
supported from the theatre gasping for fresh sea air. Small
children would, when carried away by the action, occasionally
slip through the gaps in the seating and require rescuing. The
stage floor was parquet and treacherously polished; the walls
covered in untouchable, light green flock wallpaper. All in all
an unpromising venue to present – as we saw it at the time
– new work in new ways to new audiences.

For, despite the fact that the company – the brainchild
initially of its founder, Stephen Joseph – had been running for
fifteen years, theatre in the early seventies was still thought of
largely as something done on a picture-frame stage, set apart
from the audience. Heaven knows why. The proscenium arch
was, as Stephen pointed out at the time, a comparatively
recent invention in the overall scheme of things. Certainly the
Greeks or the Elizabethans would have looked on it with some
amazement.

Here we were, then, in the unlikeliest of towns in the most
improbable of buildings presenting plays in an unusual setting
with young unfamiliar casts to largely non-theatrical audiences. I can't pretend it wasn't a challenge. When we
produced some particularly dark play – a verse drama about
a young girl's journey to suicide was such a one, I seem to

remember – on an especially bright seaside day, it was not uncommon to find ourselves performing to crowds of eight or nine.

The problem was that, on top of all the other disadvantages we were saddled with, our policy was wherever possible to present new work by new authors.

It was against this hand-to-mouth, improvised theatrical background that I was encouraged to write. First, during the late fifties and early sixties until his premature death in 1967, by Stephen Joseph himself; and then, as I gathered confidence, through my own volition.

By 1970, with seven or eight plays behind me – three of them international successes – I had taken over the Artistic Directorship of the Scarborough theatre. As a director, I was enjoying myself enormously, playing with this new toy I had somewhat fortuitously inherited. As a writer, though, I was anxious – whilst still working under the general heading of comedy – to explore fresh territory. I'd established through my earlier work (especially *Relatively Speaking* and *How the Other Half Loves*) that I could construct plays and that I could make audiences laugh. More important, they were coming back and what's more bringing their friends. Which meant that the tiny Library Theatre was now beginning to fill – not only for my plays but, as people got to hear about the company, for those of other, newer writers as well.

I wrote *Absurd Person Singular*, I remember, as I tend to write most of my plays, in a great hurry. It was due to be the second production of the 1972 Scarborough season. Before that, for two weeks in London we rehearsed, with me directing, a new version by David Campton of the classic vampire tale, *Carmilla*. During the evenings, throughout that fortnight, I wrote *Absurd Person Singular* for the rehearsing company of three men and three women. We opened *Carmilla* at the end of the fortnight for a one week pre-Scarborough 'tour' in the studio of the newly opened Sheffield Crucible Theatre. There we also started rehearsals for *Absurd* before moving on to Scarborough where, a week or so later, we finally opened the play to goodish, if not universally good, reviews.

I confess that it was, when it opened, half an hour too long. By the second night that had been remedied with some quite severe cutting. As it played in, too, it also gathered confidence and speed as the cast began to sense that they had a success. Audiences grew in size, and nightly response became increasingly enthusiastic.

Yet in rehearsal we had had our doubts – me most of all. The first act, at Sidney's and Jane's, seemed safe enough. I was pleased to have discovered the idea of 'offstage-action', to be sure. It seemed an interesting solution to set the scene apparently in the wrong room (the Hopcrofts' kitchen), in what was strictly speaking a 'backstage' area. Where we should have been, surely, was in the sitting-room. That's where the main action was happening – or so it seemed. Of course, it rarely was. The really interesting things, the things people want to say to each other in private were said in here by the sink. Besides, given that the other room contained Dick and Lottie Potter, it seemed an audience would only thank me for keeping us all out here, away from Dick's jokes.

None the less, although the act had one or two original constructional notions, it departed very little from the conventional lines of the comedy I had attempted earlier. Relating the play over three Christmases gave the play a sense of progression and, at the same time, a unity. I also liked the idea, following our glimpse of Jane's shiny, new-pin culinary unit in Act One, of setting all the acts in various kitchens. It appealed to my sense of symmetry, besides supplying further dramatic unity. In addition, it was an ideal way to indicate the different social level that each of the three couples inhabited. Nowhere in a house says more about a person's habit and background, the nature of their day-to-day existence, than their kitchen. All well and good, so far.

It was in Act Two that unknown, untried elements were introduced and fears began to arise. The idea of having the second act of a comedy centring on a woman trying to commit suicide (echoes of earlier verse dramas) seemed potentially very dangerous. Would we be accused of insensitivity and bad taste? Would the audience on the first night be filled with people trying to recover from their own unsuccessful suicide bids?

To counteract any charge that I was using human tragedy as a cheap way to get laughs – which was never my intention, of course – I resolved that, whatever happened, the humour would never be directed against the luckless Eva herself. The comedy would spring from a genuine, unmalicious misunderstanding; it would arise from the other misguided blunderers who had totally misread her intentions.

Indeed, as performances went by, I was to learn a vital comic lesson: namely that a single, truthful, serious event can become funny when set alongside a parallel series of equally serious, but contrasting events. The secret of the comedy in the second act (though I don't lay claim to having invented it!) is that all the characters – Eva, Sidney, Jane, Ronald, even the inebriated Marion – are behaving in a truthful, logical manner. All are unaware of the comedic possibilities of their plight. In order to appreciate it, they would need to be standing well back from it all; indeed, to be where we, the audience are.

More important, by taking their own situations entirely seriously, they present us with a choice of whether to laugh or sympathize: to recognize and relish or to identify and anguish. During the London run, Richard Briers, who played the ultimately crowing, vengeful Sidney with such demonic glee, told me that for every two visitors who came backstage to his dressing room, wet-eyed from seeing a performance, one blamed his or her condition on laughing, while the other blamed it on the shock of recognizing either a close relative, or worse still, him or herself.

The second act became, despite our fears, the comic high point of the play.

In Act Three, I was again moving into fresh territory. The tone here is much more muted. A cold, bleak icebox of a kitchen. A dead central heating boiler and a dead marriage. Ronald, ironically, having lost any feelings he ever had, mournfully reads a soft porn novel with little sign of pleasure. Dick and Lottie have taken away for Christmas the sons he and Marion have never understood or bothered to communicate with much.

The underdogs are baying outside. Sidney and Jane are soon to arrive and demand that the others dance, literally, to the Hopcroft tune. Geoff and Eva have, meantime, fought each other to a standstill. Eva, now withdrawn, no longer presents anyone, most especially Geoff, with a vulnerable emotional target – or, conversely, with the smallest glimmer of warmth. Geoff, for his part, is emasculated by the failure of his work and the ultimate hollowness of his sexual infidelities.

Not perhaps the most promising of material upon which to build the last act of a comedy. Yet there is laughter, if of a more salutory kind. By now, we can no longer hide the fact entirely that we are not heading for the happiest of endings. Marion's emergence like a drunken spectre at a wake provides the final bleak-comic moment. All have been brought down by a weakness in their character. Marion through her vanity, Ronald his remoteness and indifference, Geoff his sexual and professional arrogance and Eva her self-centred self-obsession.

Only Sidney and Jane survive – but at what cost? Through an increasingly loveless, unfeeling, social-climbing partnership where the pursuit of material success is everything.

And the moral? Not that the Hopcrofts of this world will always rise and conquer. They needn't. But given the world we have where materialism does often seem to matter most, given what flawed emotional muddles most of us are anyway, the odds seem stacked heavily in favour of those with the least feelings or scruples and those with the strongest, most uncaring ambitions. I wheel and deal, therefore I am. Beware: the kingdom of the Hopcroft is at hand!

> 'I mean, in this world it's dog eat dog, isn't it? No place
> for sentiment . . . when the chips are down it's every man
> for himself and blow you Jack, I regret to say.'

Introduction

Have you written any good plays lately?

To most of you that may seem rather a strange question. It might, perhaps, have seemed less strange if I had asked whether you have written any good stories or poems or even essays lately. But *plays*? A respectable number of school hours may well be devoted to reading, discussing – perhaps even performing – plays, but it is still pretty rare for students to be encouraged to write their own. Moreover, those who do – and you may well be among them – soon discover that there is more to the business than at first meets the eye.

Plays, unlike many other forms of writing, are intended for performance. They are made, essentially, not to be read but to *happen*. They involve movement, expression and gesture as well as spoken dialogue, and they have to present these elements, with the help of a variety of technical devices (scenery, costume, lighting, sound effects and so on), in such a way that the audience is drawn into their illusion and comes to believe in it as if it were reality. As well as telling stories, plays portray characters, circumstances and situations, and they do all this mainly by means of the spoken word. The skilful playwright (from the student who writes an end-of-term skit to the professional dramatist whose plays frequently find their way to the West End) is able to judge exactly what will work best in the theatre: how long the attention of an audience can be held by a single scene, conversation or speech; which parts of the action should be shown on stage and which are best left to the imagination; how to ring the emotional changes, from indignation to excitement to laughter. She knows, too, that even the most finely crafted plays inevitably change during rehearsal, that dialogue or movement may have to be modified in order to exploit to the full the potential of actors and acting area.

In short, the serious playwright needs to have a concept of performance, to have some understanding of acting and production techniques and of what happens to a play-text when it is transferred from page to stage. Which perhaps explains why – just as so many successful songwriters and composers over the years have also been skilled musical performers – so many outstanding British dramatists have also been, in one way or another, people of the theatre. Shakespeare himself was probably a bit-part actor and something of a theatrical jack-of-all-trades before he found success as a writer during the 1580s and '90s, while the eighteenth-century comic genius Richard Brinsley Sheridan – author of such plays as *The Rivals* and *The School for Scandal* – was for some time manager and proprietor of the famous Drury Lane Theatre in London. It is in this same distinguished tradition that we recognize Alan Ayckbourn today.

The making of a playwright

The greatest influence on Ayckbourn the writer during his early years was undoubtedly his mother. She was a novelist and short story writer, and it was from her that he acquired his childhood desire to become a journalist. He tells how he used to watch, fascinated, as she typed away at the kitchen table, and of how in due course she bought him a junior typewriter on which to clatter out his own tales. And although he was bitten by the stage bug while he was away at prep school (making his debut as an actor and also adapting one of Anthony Buckeridge's *Jennings* stories to be put on one end of term), a career in journalism remained his primary goal until he was in his mid-teens.

It was then, while he was attending public school in Hertfordshire, that everything to do with the theatre began to get under his skin: not just the fun of acting (mainly Shakespeare as it happened), but the fascination of the technical side of things – costumes and makeup, sets and lighting – and, above all, the enormous sense of occasion when, after weeks of intensive preparation, the curtain goes up on the first night of a production. Haileybury, the school in question, also gave Ayckbourn a heightened appreciation of the comradeship that goes with being part of a theatrical team, because a number of the productions with which he was involved went on tour in Europe and – perhaps most memorably for him – the USA.

Not surprisingly, it was to Edgar Matthews, the teacher who organized these tours, that Ayckbourn turned for advice and help when, at the end of his time at Haileybury, he decided that he wanted to make the theatre his career. Matthews responded by putting him in touch with the celebrated actor-manager, Sir Donald Wolfit, who offered him some back-stage work and a walk-on part in a play he was putting on at the Edinburgh Festival that year (1956). It was, in fact, little more than a three-week summer holiday job, but it convinced Ayckbourn that the theatre really was where he belonged. He joined the repertory company in the south coast resort of Worthing, where he did a little acting, but was chiefly occupied backstage – operating spotlights, building and painting scenery, taking on the many responsibilities of an assistant stage manager. After a few months in Worthing he moved to Leatherhead, where he was given rather more of a chance to show his paces as an actor. And from Leatherhead he travelled to the North Yorkshire coastal town of Scarborough, where he met the man who was to have a most profound influence on his career, Stephen Joseph, and had his first experience of theatre-in-the-round. (Ayckbourn tells us something of how plays were put on at Joseph's tiny Library Theatre at the beginning of the personal essay he has written specially for this edition of *Absurd Person Singular*.)

'If you want a better part, you'd better write one for yourself'

At about the time Alan Ayckbourn was leaving Haileybury and embarking on his theatrical adventures, a seventeen-year-old Salford girl called Shelagh Delaney went to see a production of Terence Rattigan's play *Variations on a Theme*. She found the piece deeply unconvincing and declared in no uncertain terms that she could do a better job herself. And so, in some respects, she did: her play *A Taste of Honey* proved to be a landmark in post-war British drama, and it continues to be performed and studied in schools, even today.

The Delaney anecdote has a parallel in what happened to Alan Ayckbourn soon after he joined Stephen Joseph's company. He had been taken on as both stage manager (he was particularly interested in working with lights and sound at the time) and actor, and, in the latter capacity, was playing the part of Nicky in *Bell, Book and Candle* by the American dramatist, John van Druten. One day, he happened to say to Joseph that he found the role too lightweight and that he would prefer to have something more substantial to get his teeth into. The reply came, 'If you want a better part, you'd better write one for yourself. Write a play, I'll do it. If it's any good.' So it came about that the nineteen-year-old Ayckbourn wrote his first play, *The Square Cat*, and had the satisfaction of seeing it performed by his fellow actors. That, of course, was just the beginning: in the ensuing thirty years, he has written no fewer than thirty-four plays, many of them major international successes.

Part of the philosophy that Stephen Joseph preached at Scarborough was that those who work in the theatre should not restrict themselves to one narrow area of expertise, but should familiarize themselves with as many of the theatre arts as possible. Ayckbourn was by no means the only member of the company encouraged to write – playwrights David Campton and James Saunders also gained early experience at the Library Theatre – nor was he the only one encouraged to try his hand at directing. But try he did, and it soon became apparent that the insight and hard work he brought to the task made him an effective interpreter of the plays of other dramatists as well as of his own. Today, his productions are as likely to draw packed houses at the National Theatre in London as they are at his home-base in Scarborough.

An actor's delight*

The following is part of an interview in which Nigel Cooke – an actor who has appeared in several Ayckbourn plays and who has also been directed by the playwright – is questioned about his experiences:

INTERVIEWER Alan Ayckbourn always lives in the hope that 'one night, somewhere, the chemistry will be right. The right cast will meet the right audience in the right theatre and something rich and rewarding will be shared between them'. What do you think he means by that?

ACTOR It is the ultimate goal in theatre to have actors and audience at one with each other so that the audience's anticipation and reaction become a part of the play itself. Both are giving and receiving in equal amounts.

INTERVIEWER How do you think this is achieved?

ACTOR I wish there were an easy answer to that. There must be a million ingredients that go into making theatre work. It's like having a party: you can organize everything perfectly with lots of good friends, food, drink, music. And yet the party might not get off the ground . . . people weren't relaxed. Another night – with the same basic ingredients – for some unaccountable reason, everything takes off. You can't have really good theatre without good

---

* The complete interview is to be found in the Longman Study Text edition of Alan Ayckbourn's play *Sisterly Feelings*, edited by Gerard Gould.

writing. One of the things that makes Ayckbourn such a good writer is that he's always aware of his audience. It's an extremely tall order to mould hundreds of different people into a whole, but it's the writer's and actor's task, and Ayckbourn revels in it.

INTERVIEWER What else do you think makes him the playwright he is?

ACTOR His characters are always identifiable and, therefore, accessible. Above all, they are real. I believe that, in varying degrees, there's something of himself in all his characters, male and female. He never allows his audience to retreat and say 'that simply wouldn't happen'. For instance, at the end of the second act of *Time and Time Again*, when Leonard, the chief character, is busy seducing his best friend's fiancée in his brother-in-law's garden pond, dressed in ill-fitting cricket wear, the audience completely gives in to it, because all the stepping stones leading up to this moment have been skilfully laid. There is a crafted logic to his writing that is perfect and that demands a perfection of playing all the time.

INTERVIEWER Please explain.

ACTOR You have to match his ear for language and rhythm. In them lie many character clues, and you have to match them as accurately as possible. You change Ayckbourn's words at your peril. A 'but' instead of an 'and' could break the logic. You must always honour his intentions. He writes *seriously* funny plays. In performance it is easy to be seduced by the audience's appreciation of the funny parts to the exclusion of everything else. You must not go over the top.

INTERVIEWER What do you mean by that?

ACTOR Overdoing an effect. If there is a legitimate laugh to be had by slamming a door, don't do it twice. The play loses its momentum, the logic is broken again, and the audience starts to watch actors for their door-slamming ability, which isn't Ayckbourn's intention.

INTERVIEWER What *is* his overall intention, do you think?

ACTOR He likes to show us what ridiculously horrible messes we make of our own and other people's lives. He likes to take a group of ordinary, ill-matched people and push them into extreme situations in which almost anything could happen – but always within the realms of credibility. . . .

INTERVIEWER What makes Ayckbourn so remarkable a director, not only of his own but also of other people's plays?

ACTOR More important than anything, he likes actors. He is always hungry for what an actor can bring to a part. He gives you free rein, space in which to breathe and expand, and actors invariably respond well to that. He is very protective of his actors. I found that, if I had a difficulty about a particular scene, he would take the pressure off me by focusing on another character's function within the same scene. This would allow me the opportunity to look at things objectively and begin to see my character's position in a completely fresh way. In an odd way, you don't know how you've been directed, but you have. You have to listen to him all the time. He can talk endlessly around the characters in relation to each other. He frequently speculates on what would have happened if so and so hadn't decided to visit so and so. Within a few minutes he's talked you through a whole new play, all the time slipping in details which are priceless in terms of value to the actor.

INTERVIEWER So how does he rehearse?

ACTOR Hard, with tons of energy (mental and physical) and a lot of fun. He doesn't do warm-ups; he doesn't improvise. He likes actors who have learned their lines as soon as possible. He will very quickly establish a basic structure of moves. These can be changed in rehearsal, but, more often than not, you realize his initial idea was the right one. He's a great technician and doesn't mind rehearsing his actors technically. As I've said, there are long chats. He has to stop himself sometimes, because, however fascinating and informative they are, he knows there's no substitute for the actor getting on and doing it for him or herself.

INTERVIEWER Are you more aware of Ayckbourn the director or the author?

ACTOR They are one. When we ask questions, it is only to gain a better understanding of the text, never to change it. We are secure in that and in the knowledge that he's watching with a hawk-eye that we're hitting the right notes at the right time.

INTERVIEWER Does this double role make for any tensions?

ACTOR Certainly none that he wilfully imposes. The only tension I felt was of wanting to do my best for him. A healthy tension, I think.

INTERVIEWER What is it like to play in the round as you do in Scarborough?

ACTOR Thrilling. It's how he conceives his plays. The audience can see everything. The actor can hide nowhere. The reaction becomes as important as the action – the audience as important as the actors. It makes for immediate and intimate playing; the audience's response is immediate. When you're in the middle of a hilariously funny scene and suddenly a character treats someone in a way which is definitely 'below the belt', you can hear the audience drawing in their breath not knowing whether what they've witnessed is funny, savage or what, then you know you're hitting the right notes. This is part of the chemistry I think Ayckbourn strives for. Ayckbourn is a serious man of the theatre whose perception of what will work on stage is extremely shrewd. In another way I see him as a small boy who sits at the water's edge lobbing in the odd firework (heavily disguised as a pebble) and watches with equal intensity the initial ripples, the explosion and then the aftermath.

A black farce

In the personal essay with which this edition opens, Alan Ayckbourn writes about the origins, structure and themes of *Absurd Person Singular*. He makes special mention of the fact that much of its humour springs from situations and events which are, in themselves, far from comic. In an interview published in 1981, he summed up this aspect of the play by saying that it is the nearest he has come to writing a 'black farce'. Indeed, much of what happens to the characters in the course of the two years covered by the action is deeply tragic – Eva, utterly dependent on drugs, attempts suicide; her husband's career collapses about his ears; Ronald Brewster-Wright retreats into a self-absorbed and uncomprehending isolation, while his wife, Marion, succumbs to alcoholism. Each of the characters is locked in his or her own bleak little world, effectively unable – in spite of superficial indications to the contrary – to relate to or communicate with the others. It is in this mutual misunderstanding in the face of deep distress that the play's comic potential lies.

Indeed, the very title *Absurd Person Singular* – for all that it originally belonged to another of his plays and was borrowed for this when Ayckbourn realized its appropriateness – sums up the point neatly: that people who, like the Jacksons and the Brewster-Wrights, selfishly isolate themselves in their own private concerns, only succeed in demonstrating the absurdity of their situations. The most obvious example of this comes in the second act, where none of the other characters (not even her husband) really understands that Eva is trying to commit suicide, or, more importantly, the psychological and emotional reasons behind her attempt. Well-meaning and good-humoured though they may be, the near-disastrous efforts of the Hopcrofts and the Brewster-Wrights to bring order to the chaos of the Jackson kitchen are entirely irrelevant to the circumstances in which they are made. Yet it is this very irrelevance which moves us to laughter.

On a rather different level, the little drama of Jane's escapade in the rain in the first act goes unheeded by both her husband and their guests. She rushes out to the off-licence half in panic, half in a spirit of blind self-sacrifice, lest she and her husband appear foolish or inadequate to their social superiors. The pain of her psychological predicament, compounded by finding the back door locked against her and having to make an entrance – attired in her outlandish raingear – through the assembled company, makes no impression on the other characters: the only comment comes from Ronald who reports, in vague puzzlement, the arrival of a 'little short chap. Hat, coat, boots and bottles. Just stamped straight through' (page 25). And all that Sidney can find to say after Jane has been subjected to a further period of exile in the garden and is standing, at the end of the scene, at the kitchen sink pouring the water from her wellies, is that his vital, business-developing party 'all went off rather satisfactorily' (page 34).

In the final act, the roles are to some extent reversed when Jane, as well as Sidney, demonstrates a complete lack of awareness of the attitudes and circumstances of the other characters. To begin with, the pair of them creep uninvited into the Brewster-Wrights' arctic home. Even when, after turning on the lights, they discover Ronald and Marion together with Geoffrey and Eva Jackson 'in various absurd frozen postures, obviously caught in the act of trying to find a hiding-place' (page 82), they fail to appreciate the fact that they are not wanted. Then it is Jane who reminds her husband of the purpose of their visit, to give the Brewster-Wrights the singularly inappropriate Christmas presents they have bought for them – a set of electrical screw-drivers for Ronald, who was all but electrocuted twelve months earlier in the Jacksons' kitchen, and a bottle of gin for his alcoholic wife.

In all their actions, the characters of *Absurd Person Singular* display a single-minded determination – a determination that frequently turns into desperation. We have only to think of the naval precision with which Sidney plans a party to impress his bank manager, Jane's insistence on cleaning everything in sight, whether in her own kitchen or someone else's, or Geoffrey's jockeying to secure the sort of commission that will further his architectural career. The critic Robert Cushman, adapting an old proverb, suggests that 'the true mother of farce is desperation'. You have only to go to a performance of Ayckbourn's play and hear the audience's uninhibited laughter at the actions and attitudes of its 'singular' characters to appreciate how much truth there is in Cushman's suggestion.

Seeing ourselves in others

Another point worth making about the title, *Absurd Person Singular*, is that it is a pun on the phrase 'third person singular'. In grammatical terms, the third person singular of the personal pronoun is 'he' or 'she'. So the suggestion seems to be that the play is about how *other people* behave: '*I* don't behave oddly or treat my friends and family unfeelingly, nor – I'm sure – do you. But *she* does, and so does *he*.'

Ironically, in loftily dissociating ourselves from the actions and attitudes of others, we are in danger of becoming, like Ayckbourn's characters, so self-absorbed that we fail to acknowledge our own weakness and folly. At the beginning of Act Two, Geoffrey Jackson announces to the suicidal Eva his plans to shack up with his girl-friend, Sally, in a way that he believes to be entirely reasonable, but we know to be crass and unsympathetic. Oblivious to the depth of her suffering, he catalogues his wife's imperfections, but makes light of his own guilt and even tries to depict himself as something of a martyr:

Other men can settle down and be perfectly happy with one woman for the rest of their lives. And that's a wonderful thing. Do you think I don't envy that? (*Banging the table*)

God, how I envy them that. I mean, do you really think I
enjoy living out my life like some sexual Flying Dutchman?
(page 38)

But in pinpointing Geoff's shortcomings, we need to take care
not to become as blinkered as he is, and fall into the trap of
losing sight of our own. It is a very short step from 'he' or
'she' to 'I', and there is more than a little of Geoff – and of
Sidney and Eva and Ronnie, for that matter – in all of us.

Ayckbourn's Englishness

The popularity of Alan Ayckbourn's plays in his home country
is partly explained by their Englishness, and *Absurd Person
Singular* is no exception. It deals with typically English people
in typically English situations and is packed with English
idioms and colloquial speech that must give translators and
readers for whom English is a second language a very hard
time indeed. Consider Sidney's rather one-sided conversation
with Ronald in Act One:

SIDNEY   But it is a matter of striking while the iron's hot
        – before it goes off the boil. . .
RONALD   Mmm. . .
SIDNEY   I mean, in this world it's dog eat dog, isn't it? No
        place for sentiment. Not in business. I mean, all right, so
        on occasions you can scratch mine. I'll scratch yours. . .
RONALD   Beg your pardon?
SIDNEY   Tit for tat. But when the chips are down it's every
        man for himself and blow you Jack, I regret to say. . .
RONALD   Exactly.

(page 27)

The characters, too, have a particular Englishness about them:

Marion Brewster-Wright, the *grande dame* with a penchant for the bottle, pretending polite interest as she makes her tour of inspection of the Hopcroft kitchen; her husband Ronald, benignly vague and practically inept, a pillar of the community to whom – as we learn from his Act Three confession – women are a 'completely closed book'; Jane Hopcroft, the suburban housewife with a mania for housework, out of her social depth with her husband's business associates and – to the very end – something of a public embarrassment to him:

SIDNEY   Look, would you kindly not argue with me any more tonight, Jane. I haven't yet forgiven you for that business at the party. How did you manage to drop a whole plate of trifle?

JANE   I didn't clean it up, Sidney, I didn't clean it up.

SIDNEY   No. You just stood there with the mess at your feet. For all the world to see.

JANE   Well, what. . .

SIDNEY   I have told you before. If you drop something like that at a stand-up party, you move away and keep moving.

(pages 81–2)

The third – and perhaps most important – way in which *Absurd Person Singular* shows its Englishness is in its depiction of the class structure. Each of the three couples occupies a different stratum of society, with the Brewster-Wrights (the upper middle-class bank manager and his wife) at the top, the Jacksons (the young, trendy, upwardly mobile professionals) in the middle, and the Hopcrofts (the lower middle-class shopkeeper and his wife) at the bottom of the pecking order. At least, this is the position at the outset; as the play progresses, fortunes change. The professionals lose their grip on things (the collapse of Geoff's vaunted super Shopperdrome is the outward and visible sign of this), while Sidney, the tradesman with an eye to making a quick profit, establishes himself in the position of greatest power. It is he and Jane in the end, and not the others, who are invited to the Harrisons' party; it is he to whom Eva is forced to turn in the hope of getting her husband some work.

The growth of Sidney's influence is reflected in the increasing success with which he meets in the course of the play in inflicting his party games on the other characters. In Act One, his well-laid plans for pass the parcel and musical bumps come to nothing; in Act Two, he moots the possibility of 'some good party game' to 'get everyone jumping about', but all the assembled company manages in the event is a desultory rendering of 'The Twelve Days of Christmas'. In the final act, however, he has everyone — however reluctantly — dancing to his tune in a game of musical forfeits; as the curtain falls, his voice reaches hysteria pitch:

> That's it. Dance. Come on. Dance. Dance. Come on. Dance.
> Dance. Dance. Keep dancing. Dance. . .

(page 92)

Structure

The recurring theme of Sidney's party games is only one of several devices which Ayckbourn employs to bring a sense of structural unity to *Absurd Person Singular*. Another is the repeated reference to George, the Jacksons' formidable, though unseen, dog ('He was only this big when we bought him, now he's grown into a sort of yak'). Throughout the Hopcroft party, Eva is constantly on edge, worrying that he will cause a public nuisance by sounding the horn of the car in which they have locked him. In the second act, however, he becomes an altogether more threatening figure, barking at every new arrival, taking a bite out of Dick Potter's leg and trapping everyone else in the Jacksons' kitchen.

The two hearty schoolteachers, Dick and Lottie Potter, like

George, are frequently heard in the course of the play, but never seen. They too provide a unifying link, a sort of running gag. Throughout much of the first two acts, we hear them distantly laughing at their own jokes, driving one character after another to seek shelter from their oppressive bonhomie in the onstage kitchen.

In his personal essay (page ix), Ayckbourn explains that the idea of setting the play in three different kitchens on three successive Christmases appealed to his sense of symmetry. It also gives the piece greater dramatic unity and a feeling of forward movement, of progression. Furthermore, each of the kitchens tells us quite a lot about the characters who normally occupy it. Jane's is modest but spotless, all stainless steel and formica, and contains a quantity of up-to-date gadgetry. The furnishings and equipment in Eva's kitchen, by way of contrast, reflect a taste for 'trendy homespun' and have clearly seen better days. Marion's is different again: though some attempt at modernization has been made, with its old-fashioned Aga range, elderly radio and substantial furniture, it retains much of the character of the Victorian house of which it is part.

I have already mentioned that one of the principal themes of *Absurd Person Singular* is the way in which the fortunes, and – to some extent – the social relations, of the characters change in the course of the action. I might suggest, further, that Ayckbourn's chosen time-frame (of Christmases past, present and future) adds a dimension of ambiguity, of uncertainty to the play. Though the first two acts are matters of record, the third is essentially a prediction. But how accurate a prediction? Is all that happens in the Brewster-Wrights' kitchen a logical and inevitable development of what occurred in the Hopcrofts' and Jacksons' respectively? Can you suggest an alternative ending?

And how about projecting the scenario a little further forward? Supposing things *do* turn out as Ayckbourn predicts next Christmas, what do you think might happen the Christmas after that? Will Sidney still be the biggest fish in this particular little suburban pond? Will Geoffrey have recovered any of his professional reputation? Will any of the men in the play have started truly to understand their wives? And whose kitchen will we visit next time?

'This is the big one'

That is how the critic Michael Billington once described *Absurd Person Singular*, the play in which Alan Ayckbourn brought his talent as a dramatist to full maturity, in which 'form and content meet in perfect harmony'. As you enjoy it – whether on the page or, better still, in performance – take a little time to savour its memorable characters, its unlikely but successful combination of hilarity and tragedy, its lively dialogue, and its thought-provoking structure. If you can do this, you will perhaps begin to understand why – for all his Englishness – Alan Ayckbourn's reputation as a playwright is now international, why his plays have been translated into some twenty-four languages, and why when, in November 1976, *Absurd Person Singular* became the longest-running current production on Broadway, the people of New York commemorated the event by renaming one of their streets 'Ayckbourn Alley'.

Some topics for discussion before reading the play

1 What do you understand by the term 'success'? Is success the same for you as it is for your friends? Is it the same for your teacher, or your parents, or your neighbours? How do we measure success in life – by how much money a person has, or how new a car, or how large a house? What kind of success do you hope to achieve in your own life?

2 How do people behave at parties? Do they act at all differently from the way they act at other times? Which sort of person, in your view, makes the best kind of party guest, and which the worst? If you have ever helped host a party, you might be able to say something about the responsibilities involved. Can you talk about the differences between what goes on at the party itself and what goes on behind the scenes? Have you ever known a party go badly wrong? Who noticed?

3 Think of a married couple you know and talk a little about their relationship as you see it. Do they have distinct and separate roles or do they share equally in everything that needs to be done? Who makes the decisions? Who does the chores? Which is the more practical partner? Which the more artistic? Are their domestic roles divided along traditional sexual lines? How do they compare with other married couples of your acquaintance?

4 Can you describe your own room at home, or perhaps the one you share with a brother or sister? How is it arranged? What kind of furnishings does it have? Is it usually kept tidy

or in a messy state? What is special about it? In what way does it reflect your taste and personality? If you had a free hand in redecorating and refurnishing one of the rooms at home, which one would you choose and what would you do to it?

5 What do you understand by the word 'class'? Has it anything to do with your education, or how much money you have, or the sort of job you do, or who your parents are, or where you live? Do you have any friends that come from a class different from your own? Does this cause problems for you? Or for them? How do you feel about the situation? Are class differences inevitable? How do class barriers compare with barriers set up by race or sex or colour or religion?

Absurd Person Singular

Absurd Person Singular

First produced at the Library Theatre, Scarborough, in June 1972 and subsequently by Michael Codron at the Criterion Theatre, London, on 4 July 1973, with the following cast:

SIDNEY	Richard Briers
JANE	Bridget Turner
RONALD	Michael Aldridge
MARION	Sheila Hancock
GEOFFREY	David Burke
EVA	Anna Calder-Marshall

The play directed by Eric Thompson
Settings by Alan Tagg
ACT I   Sidney and Jane's Kitchen. Last Christmas
ACT II   Geoffrey and Eva's Kitchen. This Christmas
ACT III   Ronald and Marion's Kitchen. Next Christmas

Time – the present

Act One

Sidney and Jane Hopcroft's kitchen of their small suburban house. Last Christmas

Although on a modest scale, it is a model kitchen. Whilst not containing all the gadgetry, it does have an automatic washing machine, a fridge, an electric cooker and a gleaming sink unit. All these are contained or surrounded by smart formica-topped working surfaces with the usual drawers and cupboards. The room also contains a small table, also formica-topped, and matching chairs

When the CURTAIN *rises, Jane, a woman in her thirties, is discovered bustling round wiping the floor, cupboard doors, working surfaces – in fact, anything in sight – with a cloth. She sings happily as she works. She wears a pinafore and bedroom slippers, but, under this, a smart new party dress. She is unimaginatively made up and her hair is tightly permed. She wears rubber gloves to protect her hands*

As Jane works, Sidney enters, a small dapper man of about the same age. He has a small trimmed moustache and a cheery, unflappable manner. He wears his best, rather old-fashioned, sober suit. A dark tie, polished hair and shoes complete the picture

SIDNEY   Hallo, hallo. What are we up to out here, eh?

JANE   (*without pausing in her work*) Just giving it a wipe.

SIDNEY   Dear oh dear. Good gracious me. Does it need it? Like a battleship. Just like a battleship. They need you in the Royal Navy.

JANE   (*giggling*) Silly . . .

SIDNEY   No – the Royal Navy.

JANE   Silly . . .

Sidney goes to the back door, turns the Yale knob, opens it and sticks his hand out

SIDNEY   Still raining, I see.

1

JANE   Shut the door, it's coming in.

SIDNEY   Cats and dogs. Dogs and cats. (*He shuts the door, wiping his wet hand on his handkerchief. Striding to the centre of the room and staring up at his digital clock, in the 'fourth wall'*) Eighteen-twenty-three. (*Consulting his watch*) Eighteen-twenty-three. Getting on. Seven minutes – they'll be here.

JANE   Oh. (*She straightens up and looks round the kitchen for somewhere she's missed*)

SIDNEY   I've got a few games lined up.

JANE   Games?

SIDNEY   Just in case.

JANE   Oh good.

SIDNEY   I've made a parcel for 'Pass the Parcel', sorted out a bit of music for musical bumps and thought out a few forfeits.

JANE   Good.

SIDNEY   I've thought up some real devils. (*He puts his leg on the table*)

JANE   I bet. (*She knocks his leg off, and wipes*)

SIDNEY   Just in case. Just in case things need jollying up. (*Seeing Jane still wiping*) I don't want to disappoint you but we're not going to be out here for our drinks, you know.

JANE   Yes, I know.

SIDNEY   The way you're going . . .

JANE   They might want to look . . .

SIDNEY   I doubt it.

JANE   The ladies might.

SIDNEY   (*chuckling knowingly*) I don't imagine the wife of a banker will particularly choose to spend her evening in our kitchen. Smart as it is.

JANE   No?

SIDNEY   I doubt if she spends very much time in her own kitchen. Let alone ours.

JANE   Still . . .

SIDNEY   Very much the lady of leisure, Mrs Brewster-Wright. Or so I would imagine.

JANE What about Mrs Jackson?

SIDNEY (*doubtfully*) Well – again, not a woman you think of in the same breath as you would a kitchen.

JANE All women are interested in kitchens. (*She turns to the sink*)

SIDNEY (*ironically*) Oh, if you're looking for a little job . . .

JANE What's that?

SIDNEY A small spillage. My fault.

JANE (*very alarmed*) Where?

SIDNEY In there. On the sideboard.

JANE Oh, Sidney. (*She snatches up an assortment of cloths, wet and dry*)

SIDNEY Nothing serious.

JANE Honestly.

Sidney goes to the back door, opens it, sticks a hand out

SIDNEY Dear oh dear. (*He closes the door and dries his hand on his handkerchief*)

JANE (*returning*) Honestly.

SIDNEY Could you see it?

JANE You spoil that surface if you leave it. You leave a ring. (*She returns her dish cloth to the sink, her dry cloths to the drawer and now takes out a duster and a tin of polish*) Now that room's going to smell of polish. I had the windows open all day so it wouldn't.

SIDNEY Well then, don't polish.

JANE I have to polish. There's a mark. (*She goes to the door and then pauses*) I know, bring the air freshener.

SIDNEY Air freshener?

JANE Under the sink.

Jane exits

SIDNEY Ay, ay, Admiral. (*He whistles a sailor's horn-pipe, amused*) Dear oh dear. (*He opens the cupboard under the sink, rummages and brings out an aerosol tin. He is one of those men who like to read all small print. This he does, holding the tin at arm's length to do so. Reading*) 'Shake can before use.' (*He does so. Reading*) 'Remove cap.' (*He does so. Reading*) 'Hold away from body and spray into air by depressing button.' (*He holds the can away from his body, points it in the air and depresses the button. The spray hisses out over his shirt front*) Dear oh dear. (*He puts down the tin, wipes his shirt-front with a dishcloth*)

Jane enters

JANE   What are you doing?

SIDNEY   Just getting this to rights. Just coming to terms with your air freshener.

JANE   That's the fly spray.

SIDNEY   Ah.

JANE   Honestly. (*She takes the canister from him and puts it on top of the washing machine*)

SIDNEY   My mistake.

JANE   For someone who's good at some things you're hopeless.

SIDNEY   Beg your pardon, Admiral, beg your pardon.

Jane puts away the duster and polish

(*Checking his watch with the clock*) Four and a half minutes to go.

JANE   And you've been at those nuts, haven't you?

SIDNEY   Nuts?

JANE   In there. In the bowl. On the table. Those nuts. You know the ones I mean.

SIDNEY   I may have had a little dip. Anyway, how did you know I'd been at those nuts? Eh? How did you know, old eagle-eye?

JANE   Because I know how I left them. Now come on, out of my way. Don't start that. I've got things to do.

SIDNEY   (*closing with her*) What about a kiss then?

JANE   (*trying to struggle free*) Sidney . . .

SIDNEY   Come on. Christmas kiss.

JANE   Sidney. No, not now. What's the matter with you? Sidney . . . (*She pauses, sniffing*)

4

SIDNEY What's the matter now?

JANE What's that smell?

SIDNEY Eh?

JANE It's on your tie. What's this smell on your tie?

They both sniff his tie

There. Can you smell?

SIDNEY Oh, that'll be the fly spray.

JANE Fly spray?

SIDNEY Had a bit of a backfire.

JANE It's killed off your after-shave.

SIDNEY (*jovially*) As long as it hasn't killed off my flies, eh. (*He laughs*)

Jane laughs

(*Suddenly cutting through this*) Eighteen-twenty-eight. Two minutes.

JANE (*nervous again*) I hope everything's all right.

SIDNEY When?

JANE For them. I want it to be right.

SIDNEY Of course it's right.

JANE I mean. I don't want you to be let down. Not by me. I want it to look good for you. I don't want to let you down . . .

SIDNEY You never have yet . . .

JANE No, but it's special tonight, isn't it? I mean, with Mr and Mrs Brewster-Wright and Mr and Mrs Jackson. It's important.

SIDNEY Don't forget Dick and Lottie Potter. They're coming, too.

JANE Oh, well, I don't count Dick and Lottie. They're friends.

SIDNEY I trust by the end of this evening, we shall all be friends. Just don't get nervous. That's all. Don't get nervous. (*He consults the clock and checks it with his watch*) One minute to go.

5

A slight pause. The front door chimes sound

What was that?

JANE   The front door.

SIDNEY   They're early. Lucky we're ready for them.

JANE   Yes. (*In a sudden panic*) I haven't sprayed the room.

SIDNEY   All right, all right. You can do it whilst I'm letting them in. Plenty of time.

JANE   It doesn't take a second.

Jane snatches up the air freshener and follows Sidney out into the sitting-room. A silence. Jane comes hurrying back into the kitchen

Jane puts away the air freshener, removes her pinny, straightens her clothing and hair in the mirror, creeps back to the kitchen door and opens it a chink. Voices are heard – Sidney's and two others. One is a jolly hearty male voice and one a jolly hearty female voice. They are Dick and Lottie Potter, whom we have the good fortune never to meet in person, but quite frequently hear whenever the door to the kitchen is open. Both have loud, braying, distinctive laughs. Jane closes the door, cutting off the voices, straightens her hair and dress for the last time, looking at a mirror in the 'fourth wall', grips the door handle, takes a deep breath, is about to make her entrance into the room when she sees she is still wearing her bedroom slippers

Oh.

She takes off her slippers, puts them on the table and scuttles round the kitchen looking for her shoes. She cannot find them. She picks up the slippers and wipes the table with their fluffy side, where they have made a mark

Oh.

She hurries back to the door, opens it a fraction. Jolly chatter and laughter is heard. Jane stands for a long time, peeping through the crack in the door, trying to catch sight of her shoes. She sees them. She closes the door again. She stands lost

Oh. Oh. Oh.

The door opens. Loud laughter from off. Sidney comes in laughing. He closes the door. The laughter cuts off abruptly

SIDNEY (*fiercely, in a low voice*) Come on. What are you doing?

JANE I can't.

SIDNEY What?

JANE I've got no shoes.

SIDNEY What do you mean, no shoes?

JANE They're in there.

SIDNEY Where?

JANE By the fireplace. I left them so I could slip them on.

SIDNEY Well, then, why didn't you?

JANE I didn't have time. I forgot.

SIDNEY Well, come and get them.

JANE No . . .

SIDNEY It's only Dick and Lottie Potter.

JANE You fetch them.

SIDNEY I can't fetch them.

JANE Yes, you can. Pick them up and bring them in here.

SIDNEY But I . . .

JANE Sidney, please.

SIDNEY Dear oh dear. What a start. I say, what a start. (*He opens the door cautiously and listens. Silence*) They've stopped talking.

JANE Have they?

SIDNEY Wondering where we are, no doubt.

JANE Well, go in. Here.

SIDNEY What?

JANE (*handing him her slippers*) Take these.

SIDNEY What do I do with these?

JANE The hall cupboard.

SIDNEY You're really expecting rather a lot tonight, aren't you?

JANE I'm sorry.

SIDNEY Yes, well it's got to stop. It's got to stop. I have to entertain out there, you know. (*He opens the door and starts laughing heartily as he does so*)

7

Sidney goes out, closing the door

Jane hurries about nervously, making still more adjustments to her person and checking her appearance in the mirror

At length the door opens, letting in a bellow of laughter. Sidney returns, carrying Jane's shoes

(Behind him) Yes, I will. I will. I'll tell her that, Dick . . . *(He laughs until he's shut the door. His laugh cuts off abruptly. Thrusting Jane's shoes at her, ungraciously)* Here.

JANE   Oh, thank goodness.

SIDNEY   Now for heaven's sake, come in.

JANE   *(struggling into her shoes)* Yes, I'm sorry. What did Dick say?

SIDNEY   When?

JANE   Just now? That you told him you'd tell me.

SIDNEY   I really can't remember. Now then, are you ready?

JANE   Yes, yes.

SIDNEY   It's a good job it's only Dick and Lottie out there. It might have been the Brewster-Wrights. I'd have had a job explaining this to them. Walking in and out like a shoe salesman. All right?

JANE   Yes.

SIDNEY   Right. *(He throws open the door, jovially)* Here she is. *(Pushing Jane ahead of him)* Here she is at last.

Hearty cries of 'Ah ha' from Dick and Lottie

JANE   *(going in)* Here I am.

Jane and Sidney exit

SIDNEY   *(closing the door behind him)* At last.

A silence. A long one.

Sidney returns to the kitchen. Conversation is heard as he opens and closes the door. He starts hunting round the kitchen opening drawers and not bothering to shut them. After a second, the door opens again, and Jane comes in

JANE (*as she enters*) Yes, well you say that to Lottie, not to me. I don't want to know that . . . (*She closes the door*) What are you doing? Oh, Sidney, what are you doing? (*She hurries round after him, closing the drawers*)

SIDNEY Bottle-opener. I'm trying to find the bottle-opener. I can't get the top off Lottie's bitter lemon.

JANE It's in there.

SIDNEY In there?

JANE Why didn't you ask me?

SIDNEY Where in there?

JANE On the mantelpiece.

SIDNEY The mantelpiece?

JANE It looks nice on the mantelpiece.

SIDNEY It's no use having a bottle-opener on a mantelpiece, is it? I mean, how am I . . . ?

The door chimes sound

JANE Somebody else.

SIDNEY All right, I'll go. I'll go. You open the bitter lemon. With gin.

JANE Gin and bitter lemon.

SIDNEY And shake the bottle first.

Sidney opens the door. Silence from the room. He goes out, closing it

JANE (*to herself*) Gin and bitter lemon – shake the bottle first – gin and bitter lemon – shake the bottle first . . . (*She returns to the door and opens it very slightly. There can now be heard the chatter of five voices. She closes the door and feverishly straightens herself*)

The door opens a crack and Sidney's nose appears. Voices are heard behind him

SIDNEY (*hissing*) It's them.

JANE Mr and Mrs Brewster-Wright?

SIDNEY Yes. Ronald and Marion. Come in.

JANE Ronald and Marion.
SIDNEY Come in.

Sidney opens the door wider, grabs her arm, jerks her through the door and closes it

JANE (*as she is dragged in*) Gin and bitter lemon – shake the bottle first . . .

Silence. Another fairly long one. The door bursts open and Jane comes rushing out

Murmur of voices

(*Over her shoulder*) Wait there! Just wait there! (*She dashes to the sink and finds a tea towel and two dish cloths*)

Ronald, a man in his mid-forties, enters. Impressive, without being distinguished. He is followed by an anxious Sidney. Ronald, holding one leg of his trousers away from his body. He has evidently got drenched

SIDNEY Oh dear oh dear. I'm terribly sorry.
RONALD That's all right. Can't be helped.
JANE Here's a cloth.
RONALD Oh, thank you – yes, yes. (*He takes the tea towel*) I'll just use this one, if you don't mind.
SIDNEY Well, what a start, eh? What a grand start to the evening. (*With a laugh*) Really, Jane.
JANE I'm terribly sorry. I didn't realize it was going to splash like that.
RONALD Well, tricky things, soda siphons. You either get a splash or a dry gurgle. Never a happy medium.
JANE Your nice suit.
RONALD Good God, it's only soda water. Probably do it good, eh?
JANE I don't know about that.
RONALD (*returning the tea towel*) Thanks very much. Well, it's wet enough outside there. I didn't expect to get wet inside as well.

10

SIDNEY   No, no . . .

JANE   Terribly sorry.

RONALD   Accidents happen. Soon dry out. I'll run around for a bit.

SIDNEY   I'll tell you what. I could let you have a pair of my trousers from upstairs just while yours dry.

JANE   Oh, yes.

RONALD   No, no. That's all right. I'll stick with these. Hate to break up the suit, eh? (*He laughs*)

So do Sidney and Jane

Marion, a well-groomed woman, a little younger than Ronald and decidedly better preserved, comes in

MARION   All right, darling?

RONALD   Yes, yes.

MARION   Oh! (*She stops short in the doorway*) Isn't this gorgeous? Isn't this enchanting?

JANE   Oh.

MARION   What a simply dishy kitchen. (*To Jane*) Aren't you lucky?

JANE   Well . . .

MARION   It's so beautifully arranged. Ronnie, don't you agree? Isn't this splendid?

RONALD   Ah.

MARION   Just look at these working surfaces and you must have a gorgeous view from that window, I imagine.

SIDNEY   Well . . .

MARION   It must be stunning. You must look right over the fields at the back.

SIDNEY   No – no.

JANE   No, we just look into next door's fence.

MARION   Well, which way are the fields?

JANE   I've no idea.

MARION   How extraordinary. I must be thinking of somewhere else.

SIDNEY   Mind you, we've got a good ten yards to the fence . . .

11

RONALD On a clear day, eh?

SIDNEY Beg pardon?

MARION Oh look, Ronnie, do come and look at these cupboards.

RONALD Eh?

MARION Look at these, Ronnie. (*Opening and shutting the cupboard doors*) They're so easy to open and shut.

JANE Drawers – here, you see . . .

MARION Drawers! (*Opening them*) Oh, lovely deep drawers. Put all sorts of things in these, can't you? And then just shut it up and forget them.

SIDNEY Yes, yes, they're handy for that . . .

MARION No, it's these cupboards. I'm afraid I really do envy you these. Don't you envy them, Ronnie?

RONALD I thought we had cupboards.

MARION Yes, darling, but they're nothing like these. Just open and shut that door. It's heaven.

RONALD (*picking up a booklet from the counter*) Cupboard's a cupboard. (*He sits and reads*)

JANE (*proudly*) Look. (*Going to the washing machine*) Sidney's Christmas present to me . . .

MARION (*picking up the air freshener from the top of the washing machine*) Oh lovely. What is it? Hair spray?

SIDNEY No, no. That's the fly spray, no. My wife meant the machine. (*He takes the spray from her and puts it down*)

MARION Machine?

JANE Washing machine. Here . . .

MARION Oh, that's a washing machine. Tucked under there. How thrilling. What a marvellous Christmas present.

JANE Well, yes.

MARION Do tell me, how did you manage to keep it a surprise from her?

SIDNEY Well . . .

MARION I mean, don't tell me he hid it or wrapped it up. I don't believe it.

SIDNEY No, I just arranged for the men to deliver it and plumb it in.

JANE They flooded the kitchen.

MARION Super.

JANE You see, it's the automatic. It's got – all the programmes and then spin-drying and soak.

MARION Oh, good heavens. Ronnie, come here at once and see this.

RONALD (*reading avidly*) Just coming . . .

MARION (*bending to read the dial*) What's this? Whites – coloureds – my God, it's apartheid.

JANE Beg pardon?

MARION What's this? Minimum icon? What on earth is that?

JANE No, minimum iron.

MARION Don't tell me it does the ironing too.

JANE Oh, no, it . . .

MARION Ronnie, have you seen this extraordinary machine?

RONALD Yes. Yes . . .

MARION It not only does your washing and your whites and your blacks and your coloureds and so on, it does your ironing.

SIDNEY No, no . . .

JANE No . . .

MARION (*to Jane*) We shall soon be totally redundant. (*She picks up the spray and fires it into the air and inhales*) What a poignant smell. It's almost too good to waste on flies, isn't it. Now where . . . ? It's a little like your husband's gorgeous cologne, surely?

JANE Oh, well . . .

The doorbell chimes

MARION Oh, good gracious. What was that? Does that mean your shirts are cooked or something?

SIDNEY No, front doorbell.

MARION Oh, I see. How pretty.

SIDNEY Somebody else arrived.

JANE Yes, I'd better . . .

SIDNEY Won't be a minute.

JANE No, I'll go.
SIDNEY No . . .
JANE No, I'll go.

Jane hurries out, closing the door

MARION I do hope your Mr and Mrs Potter don't feel terribly abandoned in there. They're splendidly jolly, blooming people, aren't they?

SIDNEY Yes, Dick's a bit of a laugh.

MARION Enormous. Now, you must tell me one thing, Mr Hopcroft. How on earth did you squeeze that machine so perfectly under the shelf? Did you try them for size or were you terribly lucky?

SIDNEY No, I went out and measured the machine in the shop.

MARION Oh, I see.

SIDNEY And then I made the shelf, you see. So it was the right height.

MARION No, I mean how on earth did you know it was going to be right?

SIDNEY Well, that's the way I built it.

MARION No. You don't mean this is you?

SIDNEY Yes, yes. Well, the shelf is.

MARION Ronnie!

RONALD Um?

MARION Ronnie, darling, what are you reading?

RONALD *(vaguely consulting the cover of his book)* Er . . .

SIDNEY Ah, that'll be the instruction book for the stove.

RONALD Oh, is that what it is? I was just trying to work out what I was reading. Couldn't make head or tail.

MARION Darling, did you hear what Mr Hop – er . . .

SIDNEY Hopcroft.

MARION Sidney, isn't it? Sidney was saying . . . ?

RONALD What?

MARION Darling, Sidney built this shelf on his own. He went out and measured the machine, got all his screws and nails and heaven knows what and built this shelf himself.

RONALD Good Lord.

SIDNEY I've got some more shelves upstairs. For the bedside. And also, I've partitioned off part of the spare bedroom as a walk-in cupboard for the wife. And I'm just about to panel the landing with those knotty pine units, have you seen them?

MARION Those curtains are really the most insistent colour I've ever seen. They must just simply cry out to be drawn in the morning.

Jane sticks her head round the door

JANE Dear – it's Mr and Mrs Jackson.

SIDNEY Oh. Geoff and Eva, is it? Right, I'll be in to say hallo.

MARION Geoff and Eva Jackson?

SIDNEY Yes. Do you know them?

MARION Oh yes. Rather. Darling, it's Geoff and Eva Jackson.

RONALD Geoff and Eva who?

MARION The Jacksons.

RONALD Oh, Geoff and Eva Jackson. (*He goes and studies the washing machine*)

MARION That's nice, isn't it?

RONALD Yes?

JANE Are you coming in?

SIDNEY Yes, yes.

MARION Haven't seen them for ages.

JANE They've left the dog in the car.

SIDNEY Oh, good.

MARION Have they a dog?

JANE Yes.

MARION Oh, how lovely. We must see him.

JANE He's – very big . . .

SIDNEY Yes, well, lead on, dear.

Jane opens the door. A burst of conversation from the sitting-room.

Jane goes out. Sidney holds the door open for Marion, sees she is not following him and torn between his duties as a host, follows Jane off

We'll be in here. (*He closes the door*)

MARION   Ronnie . . .

RONALD   (*studying the washing machine*) Mm?

MARION   Come along, darling.

RONALD   I was just trying to work out how this thing does the ironing. Don't see it at all. Just rolls it into a ball.

MARION   Darling, do come on.

RONALD   I think that woman's got it wrong.

MARION   Darling . . .

RONALD   Um?

MARION   Make our excuses quite shortly, please.

RONALD   Had enough, have you?

MARION   We've left the boys . . .

RONALD   They'll be all right.

MARION   What's that man's name?

RONALD   Hopcroft, do you mean?

MARION   No, the other one.

RONALD   Oh, Potter, isn't it?

MARION   Well, I honestly don't think I can sit through many more of his jokes.

RONALD   I thought they were quite funny.

MARION   And I've never had quite such a small gin in my life. Completely drowned.

RONALD   Really? My Scotch was pretty strong.

MARION   That's only because she missed the glass with the soda water. Consider yourself lucky.

RONALD   I don't know about lucky. I shall probably have bloody rheumatism in the morning.

Sidney sticks his head round the door. Laughter and chatter behind him

SIDNEY   Er – Mrs Brewster-Wright, I wonder if you'd both . . .

16

MARION   Oh, yes, we're just coming. We can't tear ourselves away from your divine kitchen, can we, Ronnie? (*Turning to Ronald, holding up the fingers of one hand and mouthing*) Five minutes.

RONALD   Righto.

They all go out, closing the door

Silence

Jane enters with an empty bowl. She hurries to the cupboard and takes out a jumbo bag of crisps and pours them into the bowl. She is turning to leave when the door opens again and Sidney hurries in, looking a little fraught

SIDNEY   Tonic water. We've run out.

JANE   Tonic water. Down there in the cupboard.

SIDNEY   Right.

JANE   Do you think it's going all right?

SIDNEY   Fine, fine. Now get back, get back there.

JANE   (*as she goes*) Will you ask Lottie to stop eating all these crisps? Nobody else has had any.

Jane goes out closing the door behind her

Sidney searches first one cupboard, then another, but cannot find any tonic

SIDNEY   Oh dear, oh dear.

Sidney hurries back to the party closing the door behind him. After a second Jane enters looking worried, closing the door behind her

She searches where Sidney has already searched. She finds nothing

JANE   Oh. (*She wanders in rather aimless circles round the kitchen*)

Sidney enters with a glass with gin and a slice of lemon in it. He closes the door

SIDNEY   Is it there?

JANE   Yes, yes. Somewhere . . .

SIDNEY   Well, come along. She's waiting.

17

JANE   I've just – got to find it . . .

SIDNEY   Oh dear, oh dear.

JANE   I tidied them away somewhere.

SIDNEY   Well, there was no point in tidying them away, was there? We're having a party.

JANE   Well – it just looked – tidier. You go back in, I'll bring them.

SIDNEY   Now that was your responsibility. We agreed buying the beverages was your department. I hope you haven't let us down.

JANE   No. I'm sure I haven't.

SIDNEY   Well, it's very embarrassing for me in the meanwhile, isn't it? Mrs Brewster-Wright is beginning to give me anxious looks.

JANE   Oh.

SIDNEY   Well then.

Sidney goes back in

Jane stands helplessly. She gives a little whimper of dismay. She is on the verge of tears. Then a sudden decision. She goes to a drawer, reaches to the back and brings out her housekeeping purse. She opens it and takes out some coins. She runs to the centre of the room and looks at the clock

JANE   Nineteen-twenty-one. (*Hurried calculation*) Thirteen – fourteen – fifteen – sixteen – seventeen – eighteen – nineteen . . . seven-twenty-two. (*She hurries to the back door and opens it. She holds out her hand, takes a tentative step out and then a hasty step back again. She is again in a dilemma. She closes the back door. She goes to the cupboard just inside the door and, after rummaging about, she emerges holding a pair of men's large wellington boots in one hand and a pair of plimsolls in the other. Mentally tossing up between them, she returns the plimsolls to the cupboard. She slips off her own shoes and steps easily into the wellingtons. She puts her own shoes neatly in the cupboard and rummages again. She pulls out a large men's gardening raincoat. She holds it up, realizes it's better than nothing and puts it on. She hurries back to the centre of the room buttoning it as she does so*) Nineteen-twenty-four. (*She returns to the back door, opens it and steps out. It is evidently pelting down. She stands in the doorway holding up the collar of the coat and ineffectually trying to protect her hairdo from the rain with the other hand. Frantically*) Oh . . . (*She dives back into the cupboard and re-emerges with an old trilby hat. She looks at it in dismay. After a moment's struggle she puts it on and hurries back to the centre of the room*) Twenty-five.

Jane returns to the back door, hesitates for a second and then plunges out into the night, leaving the door only very slightly ajar. After a moment, Sidney returns still clutching the glass

SIDNEY   Jane? Jane! (*He looks round, puzzled*) Good gracious me. (*He peers around for her*)

Eva comes in. In her thirties, she makes no concessions in either manner or appearance

EVA   May I have a glass of water?

SIDNEY   Beg your pardon?

EVA   I have to take these. (*She holds out a couple of tablets enclosed in a sheet of tinfoil. She crosses to the back door and stands taking deep breaths of fresh air*)

SIDNEY   Oh, yes. There's a glass here somewhere, I think.

EVA   Thanks.

SIDNEY   (*finding a tumbler*) Here we are. (*He puts it down on the washing machine*)

Eva stands abstractedly staring ahead of her, tearing at the paper round the pills without any effort to open them. A pause. Sidney looks at her

Er . . .

EVA   What? Oh, thanks. (*She closes the back door and picks up the glass*)

SIDNEY   Not ill, I hope?

EVA   What?

SIDNEY   The pills. Not ill?

EVA   It depends what you mean by ill, doesn't it?

SIDNEY Ah.

EVA If you mean do they prevent me from turning into a
raving lunatic, the answer's probably yes. (*She laughs somewhat bitterly*)

SIDNEY (*laughing, too*) Raving lunatic, yes – (*he is none too certain
of this lady*) – but then I always say, it helps to be a bit mad,
doesn't it? I mean, we're all a bit mad. I'm a bit mad.
(*Pause*) Yes. (*Pause*) It's a mad world, as they say.

EVA (*surveying the pills in her hand which she has now opened*)
Extraordinary to think that one's sanity can depend on
these. Frightening, isn't it? (*She puts them both in her mouth and
swallows the glass of water in one gulp*) Yuck. Alarming. Do you
know I've been taking pills of one sort or another since I
was eight years old. What chance does your body have? My
husband tells me that even if I didn't need them, I'd still
have to take them. My whole mentality is geared round
swallowing tablets every three hours, twenty-four hours a
day. I even have to set the alarm at night. You're looking
at a mess. A wreck. (*She still holds the glass and is searching
round absently as she speaks, for somewhere to put it*) Don't you
sometimes long to be out of your body and free? Free just
to float? I know I do. (*She opens the pedal bin with her foot and
tosses the empty glass into it*) Thanks.

*She puts the screwed up tinfoil into Sidney's hand and starts for the door.
Sidney gawps at her. Eva pauses*

My God, was that our car horn?

SIDNEY When?

EVA Just now.

SIDNEY No, I don't think so.

EVA If you do hear it, it's George.

SIDNEY George?

EVA Our dog.

SIDNEY Oh, yes, of course.

EVA We left him in the car, you see. We have to leave him
in the car these days, he's just impossible. He's all right

there, usually, but lately he's been getting bored and he's learnt to push the horn button with his nose. He just rests his nose on the steering-wheel, you see.

SIDNEY   That's clever.

EVA   Not all that clever. We've had the police out twice.

SIDNEY   A bit like children, dogs.

EVA   What makes you say that?

SIDNEY   Need a bit of a firm hand now and again. Smack if they're naughty.

EVA   You don't smack George, you negotiate terms.

SIDNEY   Ah. (*He retrieves the glass from the waste bin*)

EVA   He was only this big when we bought him, now he's grown into a sort of yak. When we took him in, he – my God was that me?

SIDNEY   What?

EVA   Did I put that glass in there?

SIDNEY   Er – yes.

EVA   My God, I knew it, I'm going mad. I am finally going mad. (*She goes to the door and opens it*)

Chatter is heard

Will you please tell my husband, if he drinks any more, I'm walking home.

SIDNEY   Well, I think that might be better coming from you as his wife.

EVA   (*laughing*) You really think he'd listen to me? He doesn't even know I'm here. As far as he's concerned, my existence ended the day he married me. I'm just an embarrassing smudge on a marriage licence.

Eva goes out, closing the door

SIDNEY   Ah. (*He puts the glass on the washing machine and finds Jane's discarded shoes on the floor. He picks them up, stares at them and places them on the draining-board. Puzzled, he crosses to the back door and calls out into the night*) Jane! (*He listens. No reply*)

Marion comes in

Jane!

MARION I say . . .

SIDNEY Rain . . . (*He holds out his hand by way of demonstration, then closes the back door*)

MARION Oh, yes, dreadful. I say, I think you dashed away with my glass.

SIDNEY Oh, I'm so sorry. (*Handing it to her*) Here.

MARION Thank you. I was getting terribly apprehensive in case it had gone into your washing machine. (*She sips the drink*) Oh, that's lovely. Just that teeny bit stronger. You know what I mean. Not too much tonic . . .

SIDNEY No, well . . .

MARION Perfect.

SIDNEY Actually, that's neat gin, that is.

MARION Oh, good heavens! So it is. What are you trying to do to me? I can see we're going to have to keep an eye on you. Mr – er . . .

SIDNEY No, no. You're safe enough with me.

MARION Yes, I'm sure . . .

SIDNEY The mistletoe's in there.

MARION Well, what are we waiting for? Lead on, Mr – er . . . (*She ushers him in front of her*)

SIDNEY Follow me.

Sidney goes through the door

MARION (*as she turns to close it, looking at her watch*) My God.

Marion goes out and closes the door

A pause

Jane arrives at the back door still in her hat, coat and boots. She is soaking wet. She carries a carton of tonic waters. She rattles the back door knob but she has locked herself out. She knocks gently then louder, but no-one hears her. She rattles the knob again, pressing her face up against the glass. We see her mouth opening and shutting but no sound. Eventually, she gives up and hurries away. After a second, Sidney returns. He has the crisp bowl which is again empty. He is about to refill it when he pauses and looks round the kitchen, puzzled and slightly annoyed. He goes to the back door and opens it

SIDNEY   Jane! Jane!

Sidney turns up his jacket collar and runs out, leaving the door ajar

As soon as Sidney has gone, the doorbell chimes. There is a pause, then it chimes again, several times

   Ronald enters from the sitting-room

RONALD   I say, old boy, I think someone's at your front – oh. (*He sees the empty room and the open back door*)

Ronald turns and goes back into the room

No, he seems to have gone out. I suppose we'd better ... (*His voice cuts off as he closes the door*)

The doorbell chimes once more.

   Sidney returns, closing the back door. He finds a towel and dabs his face and hair

SIDNEY   Dear oh dear. (*He shakes his head and returns to his crisps. Suddenly, the living-room door bursts open and Jane enters hurriedly in her strange garb, her boots squelching. She shuts the door behind her and stands against it, shaking and exhausted*)

Sidney turns and throws the bag of crisps into the air in his astonishment

JANE   Oh, my goodness.
SIDNEY   What are you doing?
JANE   Oh.
SIDNEY   (*utterly incredulous*) What do you think you're doing?
JANE   (*still breathless*) I went – I went out – to get the tonic. (*She puts a carton of tonic waters on the table*)
SIDNEY   Like that?
JANE   I couldn't find – I didn't want ...

23

SIDNEY   You went out – and came in again, like that?

JANE   I thought I'd just slip out the back to the off-licence and slip in again. But I locked myself out. I had to come in the front.

SIDNEY   But who let you in?

JANE   (*in a whisper*) Mr Brewster-Wright.

SIDNEY   Mr Brewster-Wright? Mr Brewster-Wright let you in like that?

Jane nods

What did he say?

JANE   I don't think he recognized me.

SIDNEY   I'm not surprised.

JANE   I couldn't look at him. I just ran straight past him and right through all of them and into here.

SIDNEY   Like that?

JANE   Yes.

SIDNEY   But what did they say?

JANE   They didn't say anything. They just stopped talking and stared and I ran through them. I couldn't very well . . .

SIDNEY   You'll have to go back in there and explain.

JANE   No, I couldn't.

SIDNEY   Of course you must.

JANE   Sidney, I don't think I can face them.

SIDNEY   You can't walk through a respectable cocktail party, the hostess, dressed like that without an apology.

JANE   (*on the verge of tears again*) I couldn't.

SIDNEY   (*furious*) You take off all that – and you go back in there and explain.

JANE   (*with a wail*) I just want to go to bed.

SIDNEY   Well, you cannot go to bed. Not at nineteen-forty-seven. Now, take off that coat.

Jane squelches to the cupboard

Ronald opens the kitchen door. He is talking over his shoulder as he comes in, carrying a glass of Scotch

24

RONALD Well, I think I'd better, I mean . . .
JANE Oh, no.

Jane has had no time to unbutton her coat. Rather than face Ronald, she rushes out of the back door hatless, abandoning her headgear in the middle of the kitchen table

Sidney, trying to stop Jane, lunges after her vainly. The door slams behind her. Sidney stands with his back to it

RONALD (*in the doorway, having caught a glimpse of violent activity, but unsure what*) Ah, there you are, old chap.
SIDNEY Oh, hallo. Hallo.
RONALD Just popped out, did you?
SIDNEY Yes, just popped out.
RONALD Well – something rather odd. Someone at the door just now. Little short chap. Hat, coat, boots and bottles. Just stamped straight through. You catch a glimpse of him?
SIDNEY Oh, him.
RONALD Belong here, does he? I mean . . .
SIDNEY Oh, yes
RONALD Ah. Well, as long as you know about him. Might have been after your silver. I mean, you never know. Not these days.
SIDNEY No, indeed. No, he – he was from the off-licence. (*He shows Ronald the carton*)
RONALD Really?
SIDNEY Brought round our order of tonic, you see.

Ronald stares at the hat on the table. Sidney notices and picks it up

Silly fellow. Left his hat. (*He picks up the hat, walks to the back door, opens it and throws out the hat. He closes the door*)

RONALD Not the night to forget your hat.
SIDNEY No, indeed.
RONALD (*sitting at the table*) Mind you, frankly, he didn't look all there to me. Wild eyed. That's what made me think . . .

25

SIDNEY   Quite right.

RONALD   Ought to get him to come round the back, you know. Take a tip from me. Once you let tradesmen into the habit of using your front door, you might as well move out, there and then.

SIDNEY   Well, quite. In my own particular business, I always insist that my staff . . .

RONALD   Oh, yes, of course. I was forgetting you're a – you're in business yourself, aren't you?

SIDNEY   Well, in a small way at the moment. My wife and I. I think I explained . . .

RONALD   Yes, of course. And doing very well.

SIDNEY   Well, for a little general stores, you know. Mustn't grumble.

RONALD   Good to hear someone's making the grade.

SIDNEY   These days.

RONALD   Quite. (*He picks up the booklet and looks at it*)

A pause

SIDNEY   I know this isn't perhaps the moment, I mean it probably isn't the right moment, but none the less, I hope you've been giving a little bit of thought to our chat. The other day. If you've had a moment.

RONALD   Chat? Oh, yes – chat. At the bank? Well, yes, it's – probably not, as you say, the moment but, as I said then – and this is still off the cuff you understand – I think the bank could probably see their way to helping you out.

SIDNEY   Ah well, that's wonderful news. You see, as I envisage it, once I can get the necessary loan, that means I can put in a definite bid for the adjoining site – which hasn't incidentally come on to the market. I mean, as I said this is all purely through personal contacts.

RONALD   Quite so, yes.

SIDNEY   I mean the site value alone – just taking it as a site – you follow me?

RONALD   Oh, yes.

SIDNEY But it is a matter of striking while the iron's hot –
before it goes off the boil . . .

RONALD Mmm . . .

SIDNEY I mean, in this world it's dog eat dog, isn't it? No
place for sentiment. Not in business. I mean, all right, so
on occasions you can scratch mine. I'll scratch yours . . .

RONALD Beg your pardon?

SIDNEY Tit for tat. But when the chips are down it's every
man for himself and blow you Jack, I regret to say . . .

RONALD Exactly.

*The sitting-room door opens. Geoffrey enters. Mid-thirties. Good-
looking, confident, easy-going. He carries a glass of Scotch*

GEOFFREY Ah. Is there a chance of sanctuary here?

RONALD Hallo.

GEOFFREY Like Dick Potter's harem in there.

SIDNEY Dick still at it?

GEOFFREY Yes. Keeping the ladies amused with jokes . . .

RONALD Is he? Oh, dear. I'd better – in a minute . . .

GEOFFREY You'll never stop him. Is he always like that? Or
does he just break out at Christmas?

SIDNEY Oh, no. Dick's a great laugh all the year round . . .

GEOFFREY Is he?

RONALD You don't say?

SIDNEY He's a very fascinating character, is Dick. I thought
you'd be interested to meet him. I mean, so's she. In her
way. Very colourful. They're both teachers, you know. But
he's very involved with youth work of all types. He takes
these expeditions off to the mountains. A party of lads.
Walks in Scotland. That sort of thing. Wonderful man with
youngsters . . .

RONALD Really?

SIDNEY Got a lot of facets.

RONALD Got a good-looking wife . . .

SIDNEY Lottie? Yes, she's a fine-looking woman. Always very
well turned out . . .

GEOFFREY   Yes, she seems to have turned out quite well.

SIDNEY   She does the same as him with girls . . .

RONALD   I beg your pardon?

SIDNEY   Hiking and so on. With the Brownies, mainly.

RONALD   Oh, I see.

GEOFFREY   Oh.

Pause

RONALD   Better join the Brownies, then, hadn't we? (*He laughs*)

SIDNEY   (*at length; laughing*) Yes, I like that. Better join the Brownies. (*He laughs*) You must tell that to Dick. That would tickle Dick no end.

GEOFFREY   (*after a pause*) Nice pair of legs.

RONALD   Yes.

SIDNEY   Dick?

GEOFFREY   His wife.

SIDNEY   Lottie? Oh, yes. Mind you, I don't think I've really noticed them . . .

GEOFFREY   Usually, when they get to about that age, they tend to go a bit flabby round here. (*He pats his thigh*) But she's very trim . . .

RONALD   Trim, oh yes.

GEOFFREY   Nice neat little bum . . .

SIDNEY   Ah.

RONALD   Has she? Hadn't seen that.

GEOFFREY   I was watching her, getting up and stretching out for the crisps. Very nice indeed.

RONALD   Oh, well, I'll keep an eye out.

Pause

SIDNEY   That'll be the hiking . . .

GEOFFREY   What?

SIDNEY   (*tapping his thighs; somewhat self-consciously*) This – you know. That'll be the hiking . . .

RONALD   Yes. (*After a pause*) How did you happen to see those?

GEOFFREY   What?

RONALD   Her ... (*He slaps his thighs*) I mean when I saw her just now she had a great big woolly – thing on. Down to here.

GEOFFREY   Oh, you can get around that.

RONALD   Really?

GEOFFREY   I've been picking imaginary peanuts off the floor round her feet all evening.

Ronald laughs uproariously. Sidney joins in, a little out of his depth

RONALD   You'll have to watch this fellow, you know.

SIDNEY   Oh, yes?

RONALD   Don't leave your wife unattended if he's around.

SIDNEY   Oh, no?

RONALD   Lock her away ...

SIDNEY   (*getting the joke at last and laughing*) Ah-ha! Yes ...

Jane suddenly appears outside the back door, peering in

Sidney waves her away with urgent gestures

GEOFFREY   Still raining, is it?

SIDNEY   (*holding out his hand*) Yes. Yes.

RONALD   I'll tell you what I've been meaning to ask you ...

GEOFFREY   What's that?

RONALD   Remember that party we were both at – during the summer – Malcolm Freebody's ...?

GEOFFREY   When was this?

RONALD   Eva – your wife was off sick ...

GEOFFREY   That's nothing unusual.

RONALD   I remember it because you were making tremendous headway with some woman that Freebody was using on his public relations thing ...

GEOFFREY   Was I?

RONALD   Blonde. Sort of blonde.

GEOFFREY   (*a short thought*) Binnie.

RONALD   Binnie, was it?

GEOFFREY   Binnie something. I think ...

RONALD Make out all right, did you?

GEOFFREY Well – you know . . .

RONALD Really?

GEOFFREY You have no idea. Absolute little cracker. Married to a steward on P. and O. Hadn't seen him for eight months . . .

RONALD (*chuckling*) Good Lord . . .

SIDNEY Ah – ha – oh – ha – ha-ha. (*And other noises of sexual approval*)

The others look at him

GEOFFREY What have you done with yours? Buried her in the garden?

SIDNEY (*guiltily*) What? No, no. She's about. Somewhere.

GEOFFREY Wish I could lose mine, sometimes. Her and that dog. There's hardly room for me in the flat – I mean between the two of them, they have completely reduced that flat to rubble. I mean I'm very fond of her, bless her, she's a lovely girl – but she just doesn't know what it's all about. She really doesn't.

RONALD Maybe. I still think you're pretty lucky with Eva . . .

GEOFFREY Why's that?

RONALD Well, she must have a jolly good idea by now about your – er . . .

GEOFFREY Yes. I should imagine she probably has . . .

RONALD Well, there you are . . .

GEOFFREY Oh now, come off it. Nonsense. She chooses to live with me, she lives by my rules. I mean we've always made that perfectly clear. She lives her life to a certain extent; I live mine, do what I like within reason. It's the only way to do it . . .

SIDNEY Good gracious.

RONALD I wish you'd have a chat with Marion. Convince her.

GEOFFREY Any time. Pleasure.

RONALD Yes, well, perhaps not – on second thoughts.

GEOFFREY   No, seriously. Any man, it doesn't matter who he is – you, me, anyone – (*pointing at Sidney*) – him. They've just got to get it organized. I mean face it, there's just too much good stuff wandering around simply crying out for it for you not . . .

The living-room door opens. Eva appears. Behind, Dick Potter still in full flow, laughing

(*To Sidney, altering his tone immediately*) Anyway, I think that would be a good idea. Don't you?

EVA   (*coolly*) Are you all proposing to stay out here all night?

SIDNEY   Oh, dear. We seem to have neglected the ladies.

EVA   Neglected? We thought we'd been bloody well abandoned.

GEOFFREY   Can't manage without us, you see.

EVA   We can manage perfectly well, thank you. It just seemed to us terribly rude, that's all.

GEOFFREY   Oh, good God . . .

EVA   Anyway. Your jolly friends are leaving.

SIDNEY   Oh, really. Dick and Lottie? I'd better pop out and see them off, then. Excuse me . . .

Sidney goes off to the sitting-room

EVA   And, darling, unless you want to see our car towed away again, horn blazing – we'd better get our coats.

GEOFFREY   He's not at it again . . .

EVA   Past his supper time . . .

GEOFFREY   Oh, honestly, Eva . . .

EVA   Don't honestly Eva me, darling. He's your dog.

GEOFFREY   What do you mean, he's my dog?

EVA   (*sweetly*) Your house, your dog, your car, your wife – we all belong to you, darling – we all expect to be provided for. Now are you coming please?

Ronald smiles

And your wife is looking slightly less than pleased, I might tell you.

31

Ronald's smile fades

Eva goes out

RONALD Oh. (*He looks at his watch*) I suppose I'd better er . . .

GEOFFREY Oh. Ronnie. By the way . . .

RONALD Mmmm?

GEOFFREY I wondered if you heard anything on the grapevine about the new building Harrison's having put up . . .

RONALD Oh, this new shopping complex of his.

GEOFFREY Has he got anyone yet?

RONALD What, you mean in your line?

GEOFFREY Yes. Has he settled on an architect? Or is it still open?

RONALD Well, as far as I know, it's still wide open. I mean, it's still a gleam in his eye as far as I know.

GEOFFREY Well. If you get a chance to put in a word. I know you're fairly thick with him.

RONALD Yes, of course. I'll mention it, if the topic comes up. I mean, I'm sure you could do as a good job as anyone.

GEOFFREY Look, I can design, standing on my head, any building that Harrison's likely to want.

RONALD Yes, well, as I say, I'll mention it.

GEOFFREY I'd be grateful . . .

Marion comes in

RONALD Ah.

MARION All right, darling, we're off . . .

RONALD Right.

MARION Had a nice time out here?

RONALD Oh, yes, grand.

MARION Good. As long as you have . . .

Ronald goes off into the living-room

This really is a simply loathsome little house. I mean how can people live in them. I mean, Geoff, you're an architect, you must be able to tell me. How do people come to design these sort of monstrosities in the first place, let alone persuade people to live in them?

GEOFFREY   Well. . .

MARION   Oh, God. Now he's going to tell me he designed it.

GEOFFREY   No. I didn't do it. They're designed like this mainly because of cost and people who are desperate for somewhere to live aren't particularly choosey.

MARION   Oh, come. Nobody can be this desperate.

GEOFFREY   You'd be surprised.

MARION   Anyway, it's been lovely to see you. It's been ages. You must come up and see us . . .

Sidney and Ronald, now in his overcoat and carrying Marion's coat, return

RONALD   Darling . . .

MARION   Sidney, we've had a simply lovely time. Now some time you must come up and see us – and your wife, that's if you ever find her. . .

SIDNEY   Yes, yes indeed . . .

They all go out, chattering, closing the door

Silence

After a pause, Sidney returns. He closes the door

(*Rubbing his hands together*) Hah! (*He smiles. Quite pleased. He takes up his drink and sips it. He munches a crisp*)

There is a knock at the back door – rather tentative. It is Jane

Sidney frowns. His concentration is disturbed

Just a minute. (*He opens the back door*)

Jane falls in – a sodden mass

(*Recoiling*) My word.

JANE   I saw them leaving.

SIDNEY   Yes. All gone now. They said for me to say good-bye to you.

JANE   Oh.

SIDNEY   Where have you been?

JANE   In the garden. Where else? Where do you think?

SIDNEY   Oh – I don't know. You might have been for a stroll.

JANE   In this?

SIDNEY   Oh. Still raining, is it?

JANE   Yes. (*Pause*) Sidney, if you'd only explained to them – I could've – I mean I've been out there for ages. I'm soaking . . .

SIDNEY   Yes. Well, your behaviour made things very difficult. Explanations, that is. What could I say?

JANE   You could have explained.

SIDNEY   So could you. It was really up to you, wasn't it?

JANE   Yes, I know but – I just thought that you might have – that you would've been . . . (*She gives up*)

Jane starts to peel off her things

SIDNEY   All went off rather satisfactorily, anyway. . .

JANE   (*emptying a wellington boot into the sink*) Good – I'm glad . . .

SIDNEY   So am I. I mean these people just weren't anybody. They are people in the future who can be very, very useful to us . . .

JANE   (*emptying the other boot*) Yes . . .

SIDNEY   Now, you mustn't do that, Jane. You really mustn't. You see, you get yourself all worked up. And then what happens?

JANE   Yes.

SIDNEY   Right. Enough said. All forgotten, eh? (*Pause*) Oh dear . . .

JANE   What?

SIDNEY   We never got round to playing any of our games, did we?

JANE   No.

SIDNEY In all the excitement. Never mind. Another year.
Well. I think I'll have a look at television. Should be some-
thing. Christmas Eve. Usually is. Coming in, are you?
JANE In a minute . . .
SIDNEY Right then.

Sidney goes out closing the door

*Jane stands. She sniffs. She has finished putting away her things. Her
eye lights on the dirty things scattered about. She picks up a glass or
so and puts them in the sink. She picks up the damp cloth and wipes
first where the glasses were standing and then slowly, in wider and wider
circles, till she has turned it, once more, into a full-scale cleaning
operation. As she cleans she seems to relax. Softly at first, then louder,
she is heard to sing happily to herself, and –*

the CURTAIN *falls*

35

Act Two

Geoffrey and Eva Jackson's kitchen in their fourth-floor flat. This Christmas

One door leads to the sitting-room, another into a walk-in cupboard. The room gives an immediate impression of untidiness. It is a room continually lived in, unlike the Hopcrofts' immaculate ship's bridge. While it gives signs that the owners have a certain taste for the trendy homespun in both equipment and furnishings, some of the equipment, particularly the gas stove, has seen better days. Besides the stove, the room contains a table (natural scrubbed wood), kitchen chairs (natural scrubbed wood), a chest of drawers (natural scrubbed wood) and a fridge and sink

When the CURTAIN rises Eva, unmade-up, unkempt and baggy-eyed, sits at the table in her dressing-gown. She is writing with a stub of pencil in a notepad. Whatever it is, it is difficult to word. She and the floor around her are ringed with screwed-up pieces of paper. In front of her is an open Scotch bottle. After a minute she tears out the page she has been working on, screws that up as well, and tosses it on the floor to join the others. She starts again

A door slams. From the sitting-room comes the sound of a large dog barking. Eva looks up alarmed, consults her watch, gives a moan, and quickly closes the notepad to cover up what she has been writing. Geoffrey's voice is heard off.

GEOFFREY (*off*) Darling? Eva – Eva! Quiet, George!

Geoffrey backs in from the sitting-room

George is still barking with wild glee

George! That's enough, George! Don't be silly, boy. Sit, George. Sit, boy. At once. That's a good boy. Sit. Good George. Good . . .

George has quietened. Geoffrey goes to close the door. George barks with fresh vigour

36

George . . .! (*Giving up*) Oh, all right, suit yourself. (*He closes the door, turning to face Eva for the first time*) Hallo, darling. (*He gives her a kiss as he passes*)

Eva hardly seems to notice. Instead, she sits fiddling with one of her pieces of screwed-up paper. Her face is a tense blank

God, I need a drink. You want a drink? (*Without waiting for a reply, he takes the Scotch, finds a glass and pours himself a drink*) You want one? No? (*He puts the bottle back on the table and drinks*) Cheers. I think we're running into some sort of trouble with the Harrison job. Helluva day. Would you believe I could spend two months explaining to them exactly how to assemble that central-dome. I go along this morning, they're trying to put a bloody great pillar up the middle, straight through the fountain. I said to them, 'Listen, you promise to put it up as you're told to — I promise it'll stay up, all right?' I now have to tell Harrison that his super Shopperdrome that he thought was only going to cost so much is going to finish up at twice that. He is not going to be pleased. No, I think I'm in trouble unless I can . . . Oh well, what the hell, it's Christmas. (*Going to the window*) You know, I think it's going to snow. By Boxing Day, that site'll be under six foot of slush, mark my words. That'll put us another six months behind. (*Returning from the window*) Why didn't I pick something simple? (*Seeing the screwed-up paper*) What've you been up to? (*He tries to take Eva's writing pad*)

Eva clings to the pad. Geoffrey shrugs, moves away, then turns and looks at her

You all right? You're still in your dressing-gown, did you know? Eva? Are you still thinking about this morning? I phoned you at lunch, you know. Were you out? Eva? Oh, come on, darling, we talked it over, didn't we? We were up till four o'clock this morning talking it over. You agreed. You did more than agree. I mean, it was your idea. And you're right. Believe me, darling, you were right. We can't go on. Sooner or later one of us has got to do something really positive for once in our lives – for both our sakes. And it's absolutely true that the best thing that could happen to you and me, at this point in our lives, is for me to go and live with Sally. You were absolutely right. You know I was thinking on the way home – I nipped in for a quick one, that's why I'm a bit late – I was thinking, this could actually work out terribly well. If we're adult about it, I mean. Don't behave like lovesick kids or something. Sally and I will probably get somewhere together – and by that time you'll probably have got yourself fixed up – we could still see each other, you know. What I'm really saying is, let's not go through all that nonsense – all that good-bye, I never want to see you again bit. Because I do want to see you again. I always will. I mean, five years. We're not going to throw away five years, are we? Eva? Eva, if you're sitting there blaming yourself for this in any way, don't. It's me, love, it's all me. It's just I'm – okay, I'm weak, as you put it. I'm unstable. It's something lacking in me, I know. I mean, other men don't have this trouble. Other men can settle down and be perfectly happy with one woman for the rest of their lives. And that's a wonderful thing. Do you think I don't envy that? (*Banging the table*) God, how I envy them that. I mean, do you really think I enjoy living out my life like some sexual Flying Dutchman? Eva, please – please try and see my side just a little, will you? Look, it's Christmas Eve. The day after Boxing Day, I promise – I'll just clear everything of mine that you don't need out of the flat. That way, you can forget I even existed, if that's what you want. But can't we try, between us to make the next couple of days . . . (*He breaks off*) Did I say it's Christmas Eve? Haven't we got some people coming round? Yes, surely we . . . What time did we ask them for? (*He looks at his watch*) Oh, my God. You didn't remember to put them off by any chance, did you? No. Well then . . . Have we got anything to drink in the house? Apart from this? (*He holds up the bottle of Scotch*)

Oh well, we'll have that for a start. Now then . . . (*He finds a tray, puts it on the table and puts the Scotch bottle on the table*) What else have we got? (*He rummages in the cupboards*) Brandy. That'll do. Bottle of coke. Aha, what's this? Tonic wine? Who's been drinking tonic wine? Is that you? Eva? Oh, for heaven's sake, Eva – you've made your point, now snap out of it, will you? We have lots of people coming round who were due five minutes ago. Now come on . . . (*He looks at her and sighs*) O.K. I get the message. O.K. There is no help or co-operation to be expected from you tonight, is that it? All systems shut down again, have they? All right. All right. It won't be the first time – don't worry. (*He returns to his hunt for bottles*) I mean it's not as if you're particularly famous as a gracious hostess, is it? It hasn't been unheard of for you to disappear to bed in the middle of a party and be found later reading a book. (*Producing a couple more bottles – gin and sherry*) I should think our friends will be a little disappointed if you do put in an appearance. (*Finding an assortment of glasses*) When I say our friends, perhaps I should say yours. I will remind you that, so far as I can remember, all the people coming tonight come under the heading of your friends and not mine. And if I'm left to entertain them tonight because you choose to opt out, I shall probably finish up being very, very rude to them. Is that clear? Right. You have been warned. Yes, I know. You're very anxious, aren't you, that I should go and work for the up and coming Mr Hopcroft? So is up and coming Mr Hopcroft. But I can tell you both, here and now, I have no intention of helping to perpetrate his squalid little developments. What I lack in morals – I make up in ethics.

Geoffrey stamps out into the sitting-room with the tray

(*Off, as George starts barking again*) George – no, this is not for you. Get down. I said get down. (*There is a crash as of a bottle coming off the tray*) Oh, really – this damn dog – get out of it . . .

Geoffrey returns with a couple of old coffee-cups which he puts in the sink

That room is like a very untidy cesspit. (*He finds a dish cloth*) One quick drink, that's all they're getting. Then it's happy Christmas and out they bloody well go.

Geoffrey goes out again. He takes with him the dish cloth

Eva opens her notepad and continues with her note

Geoffrey returns. He still has the cloth. In the other hand he has a pile of bits of broken dog biscuit

Half-chewed biscuit. Why does he only chew half of them, can you tell me that? (*He desposits the bits in the waste bin. He is about to exit again, then pauses*) Eva? Eva – I'm being very patient. Very patient indeed. But in a minute I really do believe I'm going to lose my temper. And we know what happens then, don't we? I will take a swing at you and then you will feel hard done by and, by way of reprisal, will systematically go round and smash everything in the flat. And come tomorrow breakfast time, there will be the familiar sight of the three of us, you, me and George, trying to eat our meals off our one surviving plate. Now, Eva, *please* . . .

The doorbell rings. George starts barking

Oh, my God. Here's the first of them. (*Calling*) George. Now, Eva, go to bed now, please. Don't make things any more embarrassing. (*As he goes out*) George, will you be quiet.

Geoffrey goes out. The door closes. Silence

Eva opens her notepad, finishes her note and tears it out. She pushes the clutter on the table to one side slightly. She goes to a drawer and produces a kitchen knife. She returns to the table and pins the note forcibly to it with the knife. She goes to the window

Geoffrey returns

Barking and chattering are heard in the background – two voices. Eva stands motionless, looking out

(*Calling back*) He's all right. He's quite harmless: Bark's worse than his bite. (*He closes the door*) It would be the bloody Hopcrofts, wouldn't it? Didn't think they'd miss out. And that lift's broken down, would you believe it? (*Finding a bottle-opener in a drawer*) Every Christmas. Every Christmas, isn't it? Eva, come on, love, for heaven's sake.

Geoffrey goes out, closing the door

Eva opens the window. She inhales the cold fresh air. After a second, she climbs uncertainly on to the window ledge. She stands giddily, staring down and clutching on to the frame

The door opens, chatter, Geoffrey returns, carrying a glass

(*Calling behind him*) I'll get you a clean one, I'm terribly sorry. I'm afraid the cook's on holiday. (*He laughs*)

The Hopcrofts' laughter is heard. Geoffrey closes the door

Don't think we can have washed these glasses since the last party. This one certainly didn't pass the Jane Hopcroft Good Housekeeping Test, anyway. (*He takes a dish cloth from the sink and wipes the glass rather casually*) I sometimes think that woman must spend . . . Eva! What are you doing?

Eva, who is now feeling sick with vertigo, moans

Eva! Eva – that's a good girl. Down. Come down – come down – that's a good girl – down. Come on . . . (*He reaches Eva*) That's it. Easy. Come on, I've got you. Down you come. That's it.

He eases Eva gently back into the room. She stands limply. He guides her inert body to a chair

Come on, sit down here. That's it. Darling, darling, what were you trying to do? What on earth made you want to

41

. . .? What was the point of that, what were you trying to prove? I mean . . . (*He sees the note and the knife for the first time*) What on earth's this? (*He reads it*) Oh, no. Eva, you mustn't think of . . . I mean, what do you mean, a burden to everyone? Who said you were a burden? I never said you were a burden . . .

During the above, Eva picks up the bread-knife, looks at it, then at one of the kitchen drawers. She rises, unseen by Geoffrey, crosses to the drawer and, half opening it, wedges the knife inside so the point sticks out. She measures out a run and turns to face the knife. Geoffrey, still talking, is now watching her absently. Eva works up speed and then takes a desperate run at the point of the knife. Geoffrey, belatedly realizing what she's up to, rushes forward, intercepts her and re-seats her

Eva, now, for heaven's sake! Come on . . . (*He studies her nervously*) Look, I'm going to phone the doctor. I'll tell him you're very upset and overwrought. (*He backs away and nearly impales himself on the knife. He grabs it*) He can probably give you something to calm you down a bit.

The doorbell rings

Oh God, somebody else. Now, I'm going to phone the doctor. I'll just be two minutes, all right? Now, you sit there. Don't move, just sit there like a good girl. (*Opening the door and calling off*) Would you mind helping yourselves? I just have to make one phone call . . .

Geoffrey goes out

Silence. Eva finishes another note. A brief one. She tears it out and weights it down, this time with a tin of dog food which happens to be on the table. She gazes round, surveying the kitchen. She stares at the oven. She goes to it and opens it, looking inside thoughtfully. She reaches inside and removes a casserole dish, opens the lid, wrinkles her nose and carries it to the draining-board. Returning to the oven, she removes three shelves and various other odds and ends that seem to have accumulated

42

*in there. It is a very dirty oven. She looks at her hands, now grimy, goes
to the kitchen drawer and fetches a nearly clean tea towel. Folding it
carefully, she lays it on the floor of the oven. She lies down and sticks
her head inside, as if trying it for size. She is apparently dreadfully
uncomfortable. She wriggles about to find a satisfactory position*

The door opens quietly and Jane enters

*The hubbub outside has now died down to a gentle murmur so not much
noise filters through. Jane carries rather carefully two more glasses she
considers dirty. She closes the door. She looks round the kitchen but sees
no-one. She crosses, rather furtively, to the sink and rinses the glasses.
Eva throws an oven tray on to the floor with a clatter. Jane, startled,
takes a step back and gives a little squeak. Eva, equally startled, tries
to sit up in the oven and hits her head with a clang on the remaining
top shelf*

JANE (*recovering*) Mrs Jackson, are you all right? You shouldn't
be on the cold floor in your condition, you know. You should
be in bed. Surely? Here . . .

She helps Eva to her feet and steers her back to the table

Now, you sit down here. Don't you worry about that oven
now. That oven can wait. You clean it later. No point in
damaging your health for an oven, is there? Mind you, I
know just what you feel like, though. You suddenly get that
urge, don't you? You say, I must clean that oven if it kills
me. I shan't sleep, I shan't eat till I've cleaned that oven.
It haunts you. I know just that feeling. I'll tell you what
I'll do. Never say I'm not a good neighbour – shall I have
a go at it for you? How would that be? Would you mind? I
mean, it's no trouble for me. I quite enjoy it, actually – and
you'd do the same for me, wouldn't you? Right. That's settled. No point in wasting time, let's get down to it. Now
then, what are we going to need? Bowl of water, got any
oven cleaner, have you? Never mind, we'll find it – I hope
you're not getting cold, you look very peaky. (*Hunting under*

43

the sink) Now then, oven cleaner? Have we got any? Well, if we haven't, we'll just have to use our old friend Mr Vim, won't we? (*She rummages*)

The door opens: Geoffrey enters and goes to Eva. Conversation is heard in the background

GEOFFREY   Darling, listen, it looks as if I've got . . . (*Seeing Jane*) Oh.

JANE   Hallo, there.

GEOFFREY   Oh, hallo – anything you – want?

JANE   I'm just being a good neighbour, that's all. Have you by any chance got an apron I could borrow?

GEOFFREY   (*rather bewildered, pointing to the chair*) Er – yes – there.

JANE   Oh, yes. (*Putting it on*) Couldn't see it for looking.

GEOFFREY   Er – what are you doing?

JANE   Getting your oven ready for tomorrow, that's what I'm doing.

GEOFFREY   For what?

JANE   For your Christmas dinner. What else do you think for what?

GEOFFREY   Yes, well, are you sure. . .?

JANE   Don't you worry about me. (*She bustles around singing loudly, collecting cleaning things and a bowl of water*)

GEOFFREY   (*over this, irritated*) Oh. Darling – Eva, look I've phoned the doctor but he's not there. He's apparently out on a call somewhere and the fool of a woman I spoke to has got the address and no number. It'll be quicker for me to try and catch him there than sitting here waiting for him to come back. Now, I'll be about ten minutes, that's all. You'll be all right, will you?

JANE   Don't you fret. I'll keep an eye on her. (*She puts on a rubber glove*)

GEOFFREY   Thank you. (*He studies the immobile Eva. On a sudden inspiration, crosses to the kitchen drawer and starts taking out the knives. He scours the kitchen, gathering up the sharp implements*)

Jane watches him, puzzled

(*By way of explanation*) People downstairs are having a big dinner-party. Promised to lend them some stuff.

JANE Won't they need forks?

GEOFFREY No. No forks. They're Muslims. (*As he goes to the door*) Ten minutes.

The doorbell rings

JANE There's somebody.

GEOFFREY The Brewster-Wrights, probably.

JANE Oh . . .

Geoffrey goes out, the dog barking as he does so, until the door is closed

Hark at that dog of yours. Huge, isn't he? Like a donkey – huge. Do you know what Dick's bought him? Dick Potter? He's bought George a Christmas present. One of those rubber rings. You know the ones you throw in the air. One of those. He loves it. He's been running up and down your hallway out there – Dick throwing it, him trying to catch it. But he's really wonderful with dogs, Dick. He really understands them. Do you know he nearly became a dog handler only he didn't have his proper eyesight. But he knows how to treat them. Doesn't matter what sort of dog it is . . . He knows all their ways. (*Turning to the oven*) Now then – oh, this is going to be a big one, isn't it? Dear oh dear. Never mind. Where there's a will. (*Removing the tea towel from the oven*) You haven't been trying to clean it with this, have you? You'll never clean it with this. Good old elbow grease – that's the way. (*She sets to work, her head almost inside the oven*) Shall I tell you something – Sidney would get so angry if he heard me saying this – but I'd far sooner be down here on the floor, on my knees in the oven – than out there, talking. Isn't that terrible. But I'm never at ease, really, at parties. I don't enjoy drinking, you see. I'd just

45

as soon be out here, having a natter with you. (*She starts to sing cheerily as she works, her voice booming round the oven*)

During this, Eva rises, opens the cupboard, pulls out a tin box filled with first-aid things and searches through the contents. Eventually, she finds a white cylindrical cardboard pill box which is what she's looking for. She goes to the sink with it and runs herself a glass of water. She opens the box, takes out a couple of small tablets and puts the box back on the draining-board. She swallows one tablet with a great deal of difficulty and water. The same with the second. She leaves the tap running, pulls the cotton-wool out of the box – and the rest of the pills rattle down the drain. Eva tries desperately to save some with her finger before they can disappear, turning off the tap. This proving ineffective, she tries with a fork

The door opens. Barking and chatter are heard. Sidney enters

SIDNEY Hallo, hallo. Where's everyone gone, then . . . (*Seeing Jane*) Dear oh dear. I just can't believe it. I just can't believe my eyes. You can't be at it again. What are you doing?

JANE She's under the weather. She needs a hand.

SIDNEY Do you realize that's your best dress?

JANE Oh, bother my best dress.

SIDNEY Mr and Mrs Brewster-Wright have arrived, you know. Ron and Marion. I hope they don't chance to see you down there. (*Turning to Eva who is still fishing rather half-heartedly with the fork*) And what's the trouble over here, eh? Can I help – since it seems to be in fashion this evening?

Sidney takes the fork from Eva and seats her in her chair

Now. I'll give you a little tip, if you like. You'll never get a sink unblocked that way. Not by wiggling a fork about in it, like that. That's not the way to unblock a sink, now, is it? All you'll do that way, is to eventually take the chrome off your fork and possibly scratch the plug hole. Not the way. Let's see now . . . (*He runs the tap for a second and watches the water running away*) Yes. It's a little on the sluggish side. Just a little. But it'll get worse. Probably a few tea-leaves, nothing more. Let's have a look, shall we? (*He opens the cupboard under the sink*) Ten to one, this is where your troubles lie. Ah-ha. It's a good old-fashioned one, isn't it? Need the wrench for that one.

JANE   He'll soon fix that for you, won't you, Sidney?

SIDNEY   Brace of shakes. Shake of braces as we used to say in the Navy. I've got the tools. Down in the car. No trouble at all. (*He turns to Eva*) Nothing serious. All it is, you see – where the pipe bends under the sink there – they call that the trap. Now then. (*He takes out a pencil*) I'll show you. Always useful to know. Paper? (*He picks up Eva's latest suicide note*) This is nothing vital, is it . . .? Now then. (*He glances curiously at it, then turns it over and starts to draw his diagram on the back*) Now – here's your plug hole, do you see, here – if I can draw it – and this is your pipe coming straight down and then almost doubling back on itself like that, for a second, you see? Then it runs away here, to the drain . . .

JANE   You want to know anything, you ask Sidney . . .

SIDNEY   And this little bit here's the actual drain trap. And all you have to do is get it open and out it all comes. Easy when you know. Now I suppose I'll have to walk down four flights for my tools. (*He screws up the paper and throws it away. At the door*) Now, don't worry. Lottie's keeping them entertained at the moment and Dick's busy with George, so everybody's happy, aren't they?

Sidney opens the door and goes out. We hear Lottie's laughter and the dog barking distantly for a moment before the door closes

JANE   It's at times like this you're glad of your friends, aren't you? (*She goes at the oven with fresh vigour, singing cheerily*)

During the above Eva writes another brief note and places it in a prominent position on the table. She now rises and goes to a chair where there is a plastic washing basket filled with clean but unironed clothes. Coiled on top is a washing line. She returns to the table. Jane, emerging for fresh water, catches sight of her

Sorting out your laundry? You're a terror, aren't you? You're worse than me. (*She returns to her oven and resumes her song*)

Eva begins to pull the washing line from the basket. She finds one end and ties in it a crude noose. She tests the effectiveness of this on one wrist and, satisfied, pulls the rest of the rope from the basket. Every foot or so is a plastic clothes peg which she removes

I think I'm beginning to win through. I think I'm down to the metal, anyway, that's something. There's about eight layers on here.

Eva comes across a pair of knickers and two pairs of socks still pegged to the line. She removes these and replaces them in the basket

There's something stuck on the bottom here like cement. You haven't had cement for dinner lately, have you? (*She laughs*)

Eva now stands with her clothes line gazing at the ceiling. There are two light fittings and her eyes rest on the one immediately above the table. She crosses to the door, clicks a switch and just this one goes out

Whooo! Where was Moses . . .? What's happened? Bulb gone, has it? We'll get Sidney to fix that when he comes back. Keep him on the go. (*She returns to the oven again, changing her tune to something suitable like 'Dancing in the Dark'*)

Eva climbs first on to a chair then on to the table holding her rope. She removes the bulb and shade in one from the socket and places them on the table at her feet. She is beginning to yawn more and more frequently and is obviously beginning to feel the effect of the sleeping pills. Swaying slightly, she starts to tie the rope round the flex above the holder. This proves a difficult operation since she has far too much rope for the job. She finally manages a knot which loosely encircles the flex. She gives the rope a gentle tug – it holds. She tries again. It still remains in position. She gives it a third tug for luck. The rope slides down the flex as far as the bulb-holder and promptly pulls this away from the wires. The holder clatters on to the table and she is left clutching the rope. She stands swaying more pronouncedly now, a faint look of desperation on her face

> *Ronald enters. Behind him we hear Lottie Potter's laughter and, more distant, a dog barking*

RONALD   Now then, how's our little invalid getting . . . (*Seeing Eva*) Oh, good God. (*He dashes forward and steadies Eva*) My dear girl, what on earth are you doing up there?

JANE   (*emerging from her oven*) Oh, no. She's a real terror, you know. (*She goes to assist Ronald in helping Eva off the table and back on to a chair*) She can't keep still for a minute. (*Reprovingly to Eva*) You could have hurt yourself up there, you silly thing.

Ronald folds up the rope, which is looped round Eva's wrist, and leaves it in her hand

RONALD   Lucky I . . .

JANE   Yes, it was.

RONALD   I mean. What was she trying to do?

JANE   Bulb's gone.

RONALD   (*looking up*) Yes, so it has. Well, you could have asked me to do that, you know. I'm no handyman but even I can change a bulb.

> *Sidney enters with a large bag of tools. Behind him we hear Lottie's laughter and a dog barking*

SIDNEY   Here we are, back again. I've brought everything, just in case. Everything except the kitchen sink and that's already here, eh? (*He laughs*)

RONALD   What? Oh, yes. Very good.

JANE   (*amused*) Except the kitchen sink. Honestly.

SIDNEY   (*noticing the light*) Hallo, hallo. More trouble? (*He puts the tool bag by the sink*)

RONALD   Nothing much. Just a bulb gone.

SIDNEY   You've lost more than a bulb, by the look of it. You've lost the whole fitting.

49

RONALD   Good gracious me. So we have. Look at that.

SIDNEY   Just the bare wires, you see.

RONALD   Yes. There's no thingummyjig.

JANE   Just the wires, aren't there?

SIDNEY   Don't like the look of that.

RONALD   No.

JANE   No.

SIDNEY   I mean, if that was to short across like it is . . .

RONALD   Yes.

JANE   Yes.

SIDNEY   You could finish up with a fuse, or a fire . . .

RONALD   Or worse.

JANE   Worse.

SIDNEY   I mean, you've only got to be carrying, say, for instance, a pair of aluminium steps across the room and you happen accidentally to knock against the wires, electricity would be conducted down the steps and straight into you. Natural earth, you see. Finish.

RONALD   I suppose that would go for a very tall man in, say, a tin hat, eh? (*He laughs*)

SIDNEY   True, true. Not so probable. But true.

JANE   Lucky it's not the war time.

SIDNEY   Oh, yes. In certain cases, one touch could be fatal.

RONALD   Better fix it, I suppose.

SIDNEY   I'd advise it. Going to have a go, are you?

RONALD   Well – I don't know. Looks a bit technical for me.

SIDNEY   Oh, no. Very simple. Nothing to it. Look, you've got your two wires coming down . . . Look, I'll draw it for you. (*He whips out his pencil again and, searching for a piece of paper, picks up Eva's suicide note. With a casual glance at it*) Nothing important this, is it? (*Without waiting for a reply, he turns it over and starts to sketch*)

Eva stares – fascinated

You've got your two wires coming down here, you see – like that. They go through the top of the plug, here – excuse the drawing, and then they just screw in to the little holes on the prongs, you see? Tighten your grubs. Screw your top to your bottom and away you go.

RONALD   Let there be light.

SIDNEY   Exactly.

Eva scrawls another note

RONALD   Oh, well, that looks – simple enough. (*He still seems doubtful*)

SIDNEY   Right. I'll get you a screwdriver and I'll get going on the sink. (*Opening his tool bag*) Now then, let's get you fixed up. What've we got here? (*He rummages through his tools, taking out a screwdriver and a spare fitting*)

RONALD   Good gracious. What a collection.

SIDNEY   This is just the set I keep in the car.

RONALD   Really? Get a lot of trouble with it, do you?

During the above Eva climbs slowly on to her chair, steps on to the table and reaches out with both hands towards the bare wires. Jane, who has returned to her oven, turns in time to see her

JANE   Watch her!

SIDNEY   Hey-hey . . .

RONALD   Hoy . . .

All three of them run, grab Eva and pull her back in the chair

SIDNEY   They might have been live.

RONALD   Yes. (*A thought*) Might they?

SIDNEY   Yes.

RONALD   Well, how do we know they're not?

SIDNEY   Check the switches first.

RONALD   Yes, well, don't you think we'd better? I mean, I'm going to be the one who . . .

SIDNEY   (*striding to the door*) Check the switches, by all means.

Sidney plays with both switches, plunging the room into darkness a couple of times

51

JANE (*during this, still with Eva*) She's got a charmed life, honestly. The sooner that doctor gets here . . .

RONALD He'll fix her up.

JANE He'd better.

SIDNEY (*completing his check*) Yes, all safe. (*He takes off his jacket and puts it over the back of a chair*)

RONALD Ah.

SIDNEY Should be, anyway. Unless they've put this switch on upside down, of course.

RONALD How do we know they haven't?

SIDNEY Well, you'll be the first to find out, won't you? (*He roars with mirth*)

JANE (*equally tickled*) You'll be the first . . .

Ronald is less amused

SIDNEY Well, let's get down to it, shall we?

RONALD (*gazing at the light*) Yes.

SIDNEY Each to his own. (*He starts work under the sink*)

JANE Each to his own. (*She returns to the oven*)

They prepare for their various tasks

This is coming up a treat.

SIDNEY Ought to get – er – Marion out here, eh? Find her something to do.

RONALD (*clearing the things off the table*) No – no. I don't think she'd contribute very much. Probably better off with the Potters. Matter of fact, she's just a bit – on her pins. You know what I mean.

SIDNEY Ah, well. Christmas.

JANE If you can't do it at Christmas . . .

SIDNEY Once a year, eh?

RONALD Not in my wife's case. Festive season recurs rather more frequently. Every three or four days.

SIDNEY (*under the sink*) Ah-ha! You're going to be a tricky little fellow, aren't you? Nobody's opened you since you were last painted.

Sidney clatters under the sink. Jane scrubs cheerfully on. Ronald sets to work, standing on the table and on Eva's latest note. He tackles his own particular job extremely slowly and with many false starts. He is not particularly electrically-minded. Eva attempts, under the following, to rescue her note from under Ronald's feet. It rips. She scrawls another rapidly

RONALD Must be pretty pleased with your year, I should imagine.

SIDNEY Beg pardon?

RONALD Had a good year. Must be pretty pleased.

SIDNEY Oh, yes. Had a few lucky hunches. Seemed to pay off.

RONALD I should say so.

SIDNEY Mustn't complain, anyway.

JANE No. Mustn't complain.

SIDNEY As long as you're looking after our money. Eh? (*He laughs*)

RONALD Oh, yes. Yes.

They work. Sidney whistles. Ronald hums. Jane sings. Occasionally, the workers break off their respective melodies to make those sounds that people make when wrestling with inanimate objects. 'Come on, you little . . . Just one more . . . get in, get in, etc.' During this Eva, having finished her note, sees Sidney's bag of tools. Unseen by the others, she goes to the bag and removes a lethal-looking tin of paint stripper. Also a hammer and a nail. She nails her latest note to the table with the hammer which she leaves on the table. Turning her attention to the paint stripper, she tries to get the top off. It is very stiff. She struggles vainly then goes to the room door, intending to use it as a vice

At this moment Marion enters

Eva is pushed behind the door, and, as it swings shut, she clings to the handle and falls across the floor. While the door is open the dog barks and raised voices are heard

MARION (*holding a gin bottle and glass*) I say – something rather ghastly's happened.

RONALD (*concentrating hard*) Oh, yes?

53

MARION Goodness! Don't you all look busy? Darling, what are you doing up there?

Eva tries to open the bottle with the walk-in cupboard door

RONALD Oh, just a little light electrical work or should I say a little electrical light work? (*He laughs*)

SIDNEY Electrical light work. (*He laughs*)

JANE Electrical light work. (*She laughs*)

SIDNEY I like that – yes . . .

MARION Yes, very funny, darling. Now do come down, please, before you blow us all up. You know absolutely nothing about that sort of thing at all.

RONALD I don't know . . .

MARION Absolutely nothing.

RONALD I fixed that bottle lamp with a cork in it, didn't I?

MARION Yes, darling, and we all had to sit round admiring it while the lampshade burst into flames.

Eva goes to the toolbag for a screwdriver

RONALD (*irritably*) That was entirely the fault of the bloody lampshade.

MARION I was terrified. The whole thing was an absolute death trap. I had to give it to the Scouts for jumble.

SIDNEY What was the trouble?

MARION It was like modern sculpture. Bare wires sticking out at extraordinary angles.

Eva goes and sits down in a corner

SIDNEY No. I meant when you came in.

MARION Oh, yes. What was it? Something awful. (*She remembers*) Oh, yes. I came for help, that's right. That dog . . .

JANE George?

MARION Is that his name – George – yes. Well, he's just bitten that Potter man in the leg.

JANE Oh, dear.

MARION Terribly nasty. Right through his trousers. Of course,

54

it was entirely his fault. I mean, he was leaping about being desperately hearty with the poor animal till it had froth simply foaming from its jowls and didn't know where it was.

JANE Oh, dear, are they . . .?

SIDNEY Yes, what are they . . .?

MARION Well, I think they were thinking of going. If they haven't gone. They seem to think he might need an anti-something.

SIDNEY Rabies.

MARION Probably. I'll see. (*She opens the door*)

Silence

(*Calling*) I say, hallo. Hallo there.

There is a low growl

Oh, dear.

RONALD What's the matter?

MARION It's sort of crouching in the doorway chewing a shoe and looking terribly threatening.

RONALD Really?

MARION I don't think it's going to let us through, you know.

RONALD (*picking up the tin of dog meat and moving tentatively to the sitting room*) He's probably all right, he just needs calming down. Here, boy boy, good boy. Hallo, boy, good boy.

A growl. Ronald returns, closes the door, and goes back to his work

No, well, best to leave them when they're like that. Just a bit excited.

SIDNEY Mind you, once they've drawn blood, you know . . .

JANE Old Mr Allsop's Alsatian . . .

SIDNEY Yes.

MARION Yes. Well, it's lucky I brought the drink. Keep the workers going. And the invalid. How is she?

RONALD Very groggy.

MARION (*peering at her*) Golly, yes. She's a dreadful colour. How are you feeling?

55

JANE   I don't think she really knows we're here.

MARION   Hallo. Hallo, there . . . (*No response*) No, you're right. She's completely gone. Poor thing. Oh well, drink, everyone?

JANE   Not just at the moment. Nearly finished.

MARION   Jolly good. (*Nudging Sidney with her leg*) What about you?

SIDNEY   In a moment. In just a moment.

RONALD   Darling, I wouldn't drink too much more of that.

MARION   Oh, Ronnie, don't be such a misery. Honestly, he's such a misery. He's totally incapable of enjoying a party.

RONALD   No, all I'm saying is . . .

MARION   Well, Eva and I'll have one, won't we, Eva?

Marion pours out two glasses

SIDNEY   (*from under the sink*) Ah!

JANE   All right?

SIDNEY   Got it off.

JANE   Oh, well done.

MARION   What's he got off?

Eva finally gets the lid off the paint stripper and is about to drink it

SIDNEY   That was a wrestle and no mistake. But I got it off. The big question now is, can I get it on again.

MARION   Eva, dear, now you drink that. (*She puts the glass in Eva's hand, removing the tin of stripper*) That'll do you far more good than all the pills and patent medicines put together. (*She puts the paint stripper on the draining-board*)

RONALD   Marion, seriously, I wouldn't advise . . .

MARION   (*hitting him on the foot with the gin bottle*) Oh, Ronnie, just shut up!

RONALD   Ah!

MARION   (*to Eva; confidentially*) You'd never think it but he was a really vital young man, Eva. You'd never think it to look at him, would you?

Marion fills Eva's glass of gin so that she is forced in her inert state to drink some

SIDNEY (*emerging from his sink*) Well, time for a break. Now then, did somebody promise a drink?

MARION (*pushing the bottle towards him*) Help yourself.

SIDNEY Thank you.

JANE I think that's about as much as I can do. It's a bit better.

MARION (*going to the stove*) Oh, look, isn't that marvellous? Look at that splendid oven.

SIDNEY Well done. Well done.

JANE Bit of a difference. (*She picks up her bowl of water and carries it to the sink*)

RONALD (*having difficulty*) Ah . . .

SIDNEY How's the electrical department?

RONALD (*muttering*) Damn fiddly thing.

SIDNEY (*seeing Jane*) Hey! Don't pour that down now!

JANE Oh. Nearly forgot.

SIDNEY You'd have been popular. (*He puts the gin bottle on the table*)

JANE I'd have been popular.

MARION Well, I'm just going to sit here all night and admire that oven. I think she's honestly better than our Mrs Minns, isn't she, darling?

RONALD Anyone's better than our Mrs Minns.

MARION Oh, she means well. We have our Mrs Minns. She's a dear old soul. She can hardly see and she only comes in for two hours a day and when she's gone we spend the rest of the time cleaning up after her. But she's got an absolute heart of gold.

RONALD Largely paid for by us.

SIDNEY Good health. Happy Christmas to all.

MARION Happy New Year.

JANE Yes.

SIDNEY Get this lot finished, maybe there'll be time for a game . . .

JANE Oh, yes . . .

MARION What sort of game do you mean?

57

SIDNEY You know. Some good party game. Get everyone jumping about.

MARION What an obscene idea.

SIDNEY Oh, they're great fun. We've had some laughs, haven't we?

JANE Talk about laughs . . .

RONALD Blast.

SIDNEY What's the matter?

RONALD Dropped the little thing. Could you see if you can see it. I've got to keep holding on to this or it'll drop off. Little thing about so big.

MARION What little thing?

RONALD A whajamacallit.

JANE Small was it?

RONALD Lord, yes. Tiny little thingy.

SIDNEY Oh dear oh dear.

They hunt, Sidney crawls on hands and knees

JANE Might have rolled anywhere.

MARION What are we looking for?

RONALD Little whosit. Goes in here.

MARION Darling, do be more precise. What's a whosit?

JANE You know, one of those – one of those – isn't that silly, I can't think of the word.

MARION Well, I refuse to look till I know what we're looking for. We could be here all night. I mean, from the look of this floor it's simply littered with little whosits.

SIDNEY (*under the table*) Can't see it.

JANE It's on the tip of my tongue . . . that's it, a nut. Little nut.

MARION (*searching by the sink*) Oh, well then, a nut. Now we know. Everyone hunt for a little nut.

Eva goes and sits at the table

SIDNEY I didn't know we were looking for a nut.

JANE Aren't we?

58

RONALD   No. A screw. That's what I'm after, a screw.

SIDNEY   A screw, yes.

JANE   Oh, a screw.

MARION   All right, everybody, stop looking for nuts. Ronnie's now decided he wants a screw. I can't see a thing, and I think it would be terribly sensible if we put the light on, wouldn't it?

RONALD   Good idea.

Marion goes to the light switch.

SIDNEY   (*realizing far too late*) No, I wouldn't turn that on . . .

Marion presses the switch

MARION   There.

Ronald, on the table, starts vibrating, emitting a low moan

SIDNEY   (*rising*) Turn it off.

JANE   Get him away.

MARION   Darling, what on earth are you doing?

JANE   (*reaching out to pull Ronald away*) Get him away.

SIDNEY   No, don't touch him, he's live. (*He goes to the switch*)

Jane touches him and recoils, with a squeak

RONALD   (*through gritted teeth*) Somebody turn it off.

Sidney turns it off

SIDNEY   All right. Panic over.

Ronald continues to vibrate

JANE   Turn him off, Sidney.

SIDNEY   I have.

JANE   Turn him off!

SIDNEY   He is off. (*Calming Jane*) Now, pull yourself together. Help me get him down. Get him down.

Sidney and Jane guide Ronald down from the table and guide him to a chair. Marion watches them

MARION   Good Lord. Wasn't that extraordinary?

SIDNEY   Easy now.

JANE   Take it slowly.

Eva pours herself another drink

MARION   Whenever he fiddles about with anything electrical it always ends in disaster. This always happens. Is he all right?

SIDNEY   He's in a state of shock.

JANE   He would be.

SIDNEY   Sit him down and keep him warm – that's the way. Pass me my jacket. Jacket. Jacket.

MARION   He looks frightfully odd.

JANE   (*bringing Sidney's jacket*) Here.

SIDNEY   He needs more. He really needs to be wrapped up, otherwise . . .

JANE   (*looking round*) There's nothing much here.

SIDNEY   Well, find something. In the other room. We need blankets.

JANE   Right.

Jane goes to the door whilst Marion looks vaguely round the kitchen

SIDNEY   Now easy, old chap. Just keep breathing . . .

Jane opens the door. There is a fierce growling. She withdraws swiftly and closes it

JANE   He's still there.

SIDNEY   Who?

JANE   The dog.

SIDNEY   Well, step over him. This is an emergency.

JANE   I'm not stepping over him. You step over him.

SIDNEY   Oh dear oh dear.

MARION   (*who has found the washing basket*) What about these bits and bobs? (*She picks up an article of clothing*)

SIDNEY What's that?

MARION Last week's washing, I think. (*Sniffing it*) It seems fairly clean. Might be better than nothing.

SIDNEY Yes, well, better than nothing.

MARION It seems dry.

JANE Better than nothing.

Between them, during the following, they cover Ronald in an assortment of laundry, both male and female. He finishes up more or less encased in it but still quivering

SIDNEY Quick as you can. Come along, quick as you can.

JANE (*examining a shirt*) She hasn't got this collar very clean.

SIDNEY Jane, come along.

MARION (*holding up a petticoat*) Oh, that's rather pretty. I wonder where she got this.

SIDNEY Not the time for that now. That the lot?

MARION Yes. Only socks left. And you-know-whats.

SIDNEY Well, it'll keep his temperature up.

MARION Oh, my God, what does he look like? Ronnie! You know I've got a terrible temptation to phone up his chief cashier. If he could see him now ... (*She starts to laugh*)

JANE I don't think he's very well, you know.

MARION Yes, I'm sorry. It's just that I've never seen anything quite so ludicrous.

SIDNEY (*moving a stool up beside Ronald*) Might I suggest that Marion sits down with her husband just until the doctor gets here for Mrs Jackson ...

JANE Then he can look at them both.

SIDNEY Precisely.

JANE Lucky he was coming.

SIDNEY Yes, well, we'd better just finish off and clear up, hadn't we?

MARION (*sitting beside Ronald*) Would you like a drink, darling? You look dreadful!

JANE   I'd better just go over the floor.

SIDNEY   (*preparing to go under the sink again*) No, dear, we don't want you to go over the floor. Not now . . .

JANE   Just where we've been tramping about. If Doctor's coming. It won't take a minute.

SIDNEY   All right. Carry on, Sister. Sorry I spoke.

JANE   (*going to the walk-in cupboard*) Now where does she keep her broom?

RONALD   (*strained tone*) You know, I feel very peculiar.

Jane finds the broom and starts clearing the immediate vicinity around the table

MARION   Well, I hope you won't be like this all over Christmas, darling. I mean we've got your mother over tomorrow for lunch and Edith and the twins on Boxing Day – I just couldn't face them alone, I just couldn't.

JANE   (*to Eva*) Excuse me, dear. I wonder if you could just . . . (*She winds up the rope, still looped to Eva's wrist, and puts it in Eva's hand*) Tell you what, why don't you sit up here? Just for a second. Then I won't get in the way of your feet. (*She assists Eva to sit on the edge of the table*) Upsidaisy.

SIDNEY   (*sliding under the sink*) She all right still?

JANE   I think so.

Eva yawns

Just a bit tired. Neglected you in all the excitement, haven't we? Never mind. Just sit there. Doctor'll be here soon. (*She sweeps under the table*)

MARION   You know, I believe I'm beginning to feel dizzy as well. I hope I haven't caught it from her.

JANE   I hope not. What a Christmas, eh?

SIDNEY   (*from under the sink*) We'll be laughing about this.

JANE   (*going to the sink and lifting Sidney's feet*) Excuse me, dear. What's that?

SIDNEY   I say, in about two weeks' time, we'll –

Jane pours the water away in the sink

– all be sitting down and laughing about – aaaah!

JANE Oh, no.

SIDNEY Put the plug in.

JANE (*feverishly following the plug chain*) I can't find the end.

SIDNEY Put the plug in!

JANE (*putting the plug in*) I'm sorry.

SIDNEY (*emerging from under the sink, his top half drenched in dirty water*) Look what you've done.

JANE I'm terribly sorry. (*She picks up a dish cloth*)

SIDNEY Look what you have done! You silly woman!

She tries to mop him down with the dish cloth

(*Beating her away*) Don't do that! Don't do that! It's too late for that. Look at this shirt. This is a new shirt.

JANE Well, it'll wash. It'll wash. I'll wash it. It's only oven grease.

SIDNEY I told you, didn't I? I said, whatever you do—don't pour water down there, didn't I?

JANE I didn't think . . .

SIDNEY Obviously.

JANE Well, take the shirt off now and I'll : . .

SIDNEY And I'll go home in my singlet, I suppose?

JANE Nobody'll notice.

SIDNEY Of course they'll notice. Otherwise, there'd be no point in wearing a shirt in the first place, would there? If nobody noticed, we'd all be walking around in our singlets.

JANE It's dark.

SIDNEY Don't change the subject. It would really teach you a lesson if I caught pneumonia.

JANE (*tearful*) Don't say that.

SIDNEY Teach you, that would.

Jane sniffs. Sidney strides to the door

Dear oh dear.

63

JANE   (*following him*) Where are you going?

SIDNEY   To get my overcoat before I freeze. Where else do you think I'm going?

JANE   But, Sidney . . .

Sidney ignores her, flinging open the door and striding out, making a dignified exit. There is a burst of furious barking. Sidney reappears very swiftly and closes the door behind him

SIDNEY   (*to Eva; furiously*) That dog of yours is a liability. You ought to keep that animal under control. I can't even get to my overcoat. It's not good enough.

Eva slowly lies down on the kitchen table, oblivious

JANE   Come and sit down.

SIDNEY   Sit down? What's the point of sitting down?

JANE   Geoff should be back soon.

SIDNEY   I should hope so. This isn't what you expect at all. Not when you come round for a quiet drink and a chat. (*Almost screaming in Eva's ear*) This is the last time I accept hospitality in this household.

JANE   Ssh.

SIDNEY   What?

JANE   She'll hear you.

SIDNEY   I don't care who hears me. (*He sits*)

JANE   Ssh. (*She sits*)

A pause. The four of them are sitting. Eva lies. Ronald continues to look glassy, quivering slightly; Marion's drinking has caught up with her. Jane looks abjectly miserable. Sidney shivers in his vest.

SIDNEY   And we're missing the television.

JANE   Ssh.

A silence. Then, from apparently nowhere, a sleepy voice begins to sing dreamily. It is Eva

EVA   (*singing*) 'On the first day of Christmas my true love sent to me, a partridge in a pear tree. On the second

day of Christmas my true love sent to me, two turtle
doves –

MARION   (*joining her*) – and a partridge in a pear tree. On the
third day of Christmas my true love sent to me, three French
hens –

JANE   (*joining her*) – two turtle doves and a partridge in a pear
tree. On the fourth day of Christmas my true love sent to
me, four calling birds –

RONALD   (*joining them*) – three French hens, two turtle doves
and a partridge in a pear tree.

ALL   On the fifth day of Christmas my true love sent to me, five
gold rings, etc.

*As the bedraggled quintet begin to open up, the singing gets bolder and
more confident. Somewhere in the distance George begins to howl. Eva,
still lying on her back, conducts them dreamily with both hands and then
finally with the hammer*

The door bursts open. Geoffrey enters hurriedly, calling behind him

GEOFFREY   Through here, Doctor. Please hurry, I . . .

*Geoffrey is suddenly aware of the sound behind him. He turns, still
breathless from his run up four flights. His mouth drops further open
as he surveys the scene. The singing continues unabated, as the Lights
black-out and –*

the CURTAIN *falls*

Act Three

The Brewster-Wrights' kitchen. Next Christmas

They live in a big old Victorian house, and the kitchen, though modernized to some extent, still retains a lot of the flavour of the original room. A sink, an electric stove (or even an Aga range), a fridge, a dark wood sideboard, a round table and chairs form the substantial furnishings for the room. On the table is an elderly radio set. There is a door, half of opaque glass, to the hall, and a garden door

When the CURTAIN rises, Ronald is discovered sitting in an armchair near the table. He wears a scarf and a green eye-shade. Beside him is a lighted portable oil stove. At his elbow is an empty teacup. The radio is on, playing very quietly a very jolly carol. Ronald is reading a book. He is obviously enjoying it, for every two or three seconds he chuckles to himself out loud. This continues for some seconds, until the door from the hall opens and Eva enters. She wears a winter coat and carries an empty teacup and plate, which she puts down on the draining-board

RONALD Oh. Hallo there.

EVA All right?

RONALD Oh, yes. (*He switches off the radio*)

EVA Are you warm enough in here?

RONALD Oh, yes. It's fine in here. Well, not too bad.

EVA The rest of the house is freezing. I don't envy you going to bed.

RONALD Her room's all right, though, is it?

EVA Oh, she's got three electric fires blazing away.

RONALD My God. That'll be the second power station I've paid for this winter.

EVA She seems to be rather dug in up there. Almost in a state of hibernation. Doesn't she ever come out?

RONALD Not if she can help it. Heating system went on the blink, you see – usual thing and we had a few frosty words over it and – the outcome was, she said she wasn't setting foot outside her room until I got it fixed.

EVA (*putting on a pair of gloves*) Well, how long's it been like this?

RONALD (*vaguely*) Oh, I don't know. Two or three weeks, I suppose.

EVA Well, that's disgusting. Can't you get the men round to fix it?

RONALD Yes, yes. I have phoned them several times. But I've been a bit unlucky up to now. They always seem to be at lunch . . .

EVA (*taking off her coat and putting it on the back of a chair*) Well, I wouldn't put up with it. I'd scream the place down till Geoffrey got it fixed. (*She hunts in the cupboards*)

RONALD Yes, we've had a packet of trouble with this central heating. Always goes on the blink. Either the day before Christmas, the day before Easter or the day before Whitsun. Always seems to manage it. Don't understand the principle it works on but whatever it is, seems to be very closely tied in with the Church calendar. (*He laughs*) Can I help you at all?

EVA She said she'd like a sandwich. (*She puts a plate, knife, bread and a pot of peanut butter on a bread board*)

RONALD (*looking at his watch*) Oh, yes. She's about due for a sandwich.

EVA I'm looking for the butter.

RONALD Oh. don't you bother to do that, I'll . . .

EVA It's all right. Where do you keep your butter?

RONALD Do you know, that's very interesting. I have absolutely no idea. A closely guarded secret kept by Mrs Minns. I suppose we could hazard a guess. Now then, butter. Try the fridge.

EVA Fridge?

RONALD Keeps it soft. It's warmer in there than it is outside.

EVA (*looking in the fridge*) Right first time. (*She sets about making a sandwich, taking off one glove*)

67

RONALD What's she want? Peanut butter?

EVA Apparently.

RONALD Good grief. She's got an absolute craving for that stuff lately. That and cheese footballs. All most alarming. She's not up there knitting little blue bootees, by any chance?

EVA Not that I noticed.

RONALD Thank God for that.

EVA She looks a lot better than when I last saw her, anyway.

RONALD Really? Yes, yes. Well, she got a bit overtired, I think. Principally.

EVA Geoff'll be here in a minute to pick me up. I'll get out of your way. I just heard Marion was – I hope you didn't mind . . .

RONALD No, very good of you to look round. Sure she appreciated it. She doesn't get many visitors. Lottie Potter looked in briefly. That set her back a couple of weeks. No, the trouble with Marion you see, is she lives on her nerves. Far too much.

EVA Marion does?

RONALD Oh, yes. Very nervous, insecure sort of person basically, you know.

EVA Really?

RONALD That surprises you, does it? Well, I've got a pretty thorough working knowledge of her now, you know. I mean, she's calmer than she was. When I first met her she was really one of the jumpiest girls you could ever hope to meet. Still, as I say, she's much calmer since she's been with me. If I've done nothing else for her, I've acted as a sort of sedative.

EVA You don't think that a lot of her trouble may be – drink?

RONALD Drink? No, I don't honestly think so. She's always liked a – I mean, the doctor did say she should lay off. But that was only because it was acting as a stimulant. She hasn't touched it lately.

EVA She has this evening.

RONALD   Really?

EVA   Yes.

RONALD   Well, you do surprise me.

EVA   She's got quite a collection up there.

RONALD   Oh, has she? Has she now?

EVA   Didn't you know?

RONALD   Well, I don't often have much cause to go into her room these days. She likes her privacy, you see. And I respect that. Not that it's not a mutual arrangement, you understand. I mean, she doesn't particularly choose to come into my room either. So it works out rather conveniently. On the whole.

EVA   Do you ever see each other at all?

RONALD   Good Lord, it's not as if we aren't in the same house. We bang into each other quite frequently. It's not always as quiet as this, believe me. In the holidays we've got the boys here. They thump about. No end of a racket. Boys, of course. Mind you, they're no trouble –they're usually out, too, most of the time – with their friends.

EVA   Pity they're not with you for Christmas.

RONALD   Oh well, it's greatly over-estimated, this Christmas business. That reminds me, would you like a drink? Seeing as it's Christmas.

EVA   No, I don't think so.

RONALD   Oh, go on. Just one. With me, for Christmas.

EVA   Well – all right, a little one.

RONALD   Right. (*He rises*) Good. I'll brave the elements then and try and make it as far as the sitting-room . . . .

The doorbell rings

EVA   That's probably Geoff.

RONALD   (*opening the door*) I'll let him in, then. (*Stopping short*) Good Lord, is that dust on the hall table or frost? Won't be a minute.

Ronald goes out

69

Eva, alone, looks round the room rather sadly. She leaves the sandwich and plate on the table, puts the other things back on the sideboard, returns to the table, sits and starts to eat the sandwich

Geoffrey enters in his overcoat

GEOFFREY   Blimey. Why aren't you sitting in the garden, it's warmer.

EVA   Hullo.

GEOFFREY   Ready then?

EVA   I'm just going to have a drink with Ronnie.

GEOFFREY   Oh. And how is *she*?

EVA   Drunk.

GEOFFREY   God.

Pause. Eva munches

EVA   How did you get on?

GEOFFREY   Well . . .

EVA   Did you ask him?

GEOFFREY   Well . . .

EVA   You didn't.

Geoffrey does not reply

You didn't damn well ask him.

GEOFFREY   It's no good. I find it impossible to ask people for money.

Eva gives a short laugh

I'm sorry.

EVA   He owes it you. You're not asking him a favour, you know. He owes it you.

GEOFFREY   I know.

EVA   Well then.

GEOFFREY   It doesn't matter.

EVA   Oh, my . . . Oh well, I'll have to get in touch with him then. After Christmas. I don't mind doing it.

GEOFFREY   You don't have to do that.

EVA   Well, somebody has to, darling. Don't they?

The door opens. A drinks trolley enters followed by Ronald

RONALD   Here we come. The Trans-Siberian Express. Thank you so much. We seem to be a bit depleted on the old alcohol stakes. Odd, thought I'd stocked up only recently. Probably old Mrs Minns been knocking them off, eh? The woman must have some vices. She hasn't got much else to recommend her. Now what are we having? Eva?

EVA   Could I have just a bitter lemon?

RONALD   Good gracious, nothing stronger?

EVA   Not just now.

RONALD   Well, if that's what you want . . . Geoff, what about you?

GEOFFREY   I think I'd like the same, actually.

RONALD   What? A bitter lemon?

GEOFFREY   Just what I feel like.

RONALD   You won't last through Christmas at that rate. (*Inspecting his trolley*) Well, that seems to be the only thing I haven't brought.

EVA   Oh well, it doesn't matter. Something else.

RONALD   No, no. I'll get it, I'll get it. We've got some somewhere.

Ronald goes out, closing the door

EVA   I mean, either you want me to help you or you don't.

GEOFFREY   Yes.

EVA   I mean, if you don't, just say so. I don't particularly enjoy working in that dark little office of yours. You're a terrible employer. You come in late even when I drive you to work. You take four-hour lunch breaks and then expect me to do all your damn typing at five o'clock in the evening.

GEOFFREY   That's the way I do business.

EVA   Not with me you don't.

GEOFFREY   That's what you're paid for.

EVA   That's what I'm what?

71

GEOFFREY   Look, if you don't like the job . . . .

EVA   You asked me to help you. Now, if you didn't mean that, that's a different matter.

GEOFFREY   Well yes, I did, but . . . .

EVA   All right, then. That's settled. You asked me to help you. I am bloody well going to help you.

GEOFFREY   O.K. O.K., thanks.

EVA   Not at all. (*A slight pause*) And you're not going to ask for the money?

GEOFFREY   No.

EVA   Even though we're owed it?

GEOFFREY   No.

EVA   And you won't let me ask?

GEOFFREY   No.

EVA   All right. Then we'll have to think of something else.

GEOFFREY   Exactly.

EVA   I'll phone Sidney Hopcroft after Christmas and talk to him.

GEOFFREY   Sidney Hopcroft.

EVA   He's always asking if you're interested.

GEOFFREY   If you think I'm going to get myself involved in his seedy little schemes . . . .

EVA   Why not?

GEOFFREY   Have you seen the buildings he's putting up? Half his tenants are asking to be re-housed and they haven't even moved in yet.

EVA   Darling, I hate to remind you but ever since the ceiling of the Harrison building caved in and nearly killed the manager, Sidney Hopcroft is about your only hope of surviving as an architect in this city.

GEOFFREY   I can do without Sidney Hopcroft, thank you very much.

The door opens. Ronald enters with two bottles of bitter lemon

RONALD   Here we are. Two very bitter lemons. (*He pours out two bitter lemons and a Scotch*)

EVA   Thank you.

RONALD   I think I'm going to have something more than that, if you'll excuse me. Bit quieter than last Christmas, eh?

GEOFFREY   What?

RONALD   Last Christmas. Remember that? Round at your place?

GEOFFREY   Yes.

EVA   Yes.

RONALD   Good gracious me. You have to laugh now. Old Hopcroft. (*He laughs*) Always remember old Hopcroft. Doing very well. Did you know that? Doing frightfully well. Seems to have a flair for it. Wouldn't think so to look at him. Always found him a bit unprepossessing. Still – the chap to keep in with. The rate he's going.

EVA   Yes.

GEOFFREY   (*picking up Ronald's book*) Is this good?

RONALD   Oh, yes. Yes, quite good. Very amusing. Bit – saucy, in parts. Mrs Minns found it under one of the boys' mattresses. Nearly finished her there and then, poor old thing. Bitter lemon.

EVA   Thanks.

RONALD   Bitter lemon.

GEOFFREY   Thank you.

RONALD   (*raising his glass of Scotch*) Well, Happy Christmas. Good health. God bless.

EVA   Happy Christmas.

GEOFFREY   Happy Christmas.

RONALD   (*after a pause*) Sorry to hear about your problems, Geoff.

GEOFFREY   How do you mean?

RONALD   I meant, the Harrison thing. Hear it fell through ... Oh, I'm sorry, perhaps that's the wrong expression to use – bit unfortunate.

GEOFFREY   That's all right.

EVA   It wasn't actually Geoff's fault.

RONALD   No, no, I'm sure – knowing Geoff. Unthinkable. I

mean, that local paper's as biased as hell. I refused to read that particular article. So did all my friends.

EVA   (*after a pause*) Just because Geoffrey was doing something totally new for a change . . .

GEOFFREY   How's the bank doing, then?

RONALD   Oh, well. We're not in the red, yet. No thanks to me, mind you.

A bell rings

GEOFFREY   Is that the front door?

RONALD   No. It's the – er – bedroom bell, actually. We've never bothered to have them taken out. They always come in useful. Boys with measles and so on.

EVA   Shall I go up to her?

RONALD   No, no, I'll . . .

EVA   No, it's all right. I don't mind . . .

RONALD   Well, that's very good of you. Probably nothing important. Wants the page of her magazine turning over or something.

EVA   I hope not.

RONALD   What's the harm, I say. As long as it keeps her happy.

EVA   Yes.

Eva goes out, closing the door

RONALD   I mean, who are we to argue with a woman, eh? You can never win. Hopeless. Mind you, I'm talking to the wrong chap, aren't I?

GEOFFREY   What?

RONALD   I mean you seem to do better than most of us.

GEOFFREY   Oh, yes. (*He sits in the armchair*)

RONALD   You seem to have got things pretty well organized on the home front. (*He laughs*)

GEOFFREY   Well, it's just a matter of knowing . . .

RONALD   Ah yes, that's the point. I never really have. Not really. I mean, take my first wife. Distinguished-looking woman. Very charming. Seemed pretty happy on the whole. Then one day, she suddenly ups and offs and goes. Quite amazing. I mean, I had literally no idea she was going to. I mean, we had the flat over the bank at the time, so it wasn't as if I was even very far away and on this particular day, I came up for lunch and she'd laid on her usual splendid meal. I mean I had absolutely no complaints about that. I think my very words were something like, jolly nice that, see you this evening. And when we knocked off for tea, I came upstairs and she'd just taken off. Well, I hunted about for a bit in case she'd got knocked down or gone shopping and lost her memory or something and then she wrote, some time later, and said she'd had enough. So I was forced to call it a day. Some time later again, I took up tennis to forget her and married Marion. Of course, that's all forgotten now. All the same, sometimes in the evening I can't help sitting here and trying to work it all out. I mean, something happened. Something must have happened. I'm just not sure what. Anyway. Under the bridge, eh? All I'm saying really, is some people seem to have the hang of it and some of us just aren't so lucky.

GEOFFREY   Hang of what?

RONALD   Well – this whole women business, really. I mean, this may sound ridiculous, but I've never to this day really known what most women think about anything. Completely closed book to me. I mean, God bless them, what would we do without them? But I've never understood them. I mean, damn it all, one minute you're having a perfectly good time and the next, you suddenly see them there like – some old sports jacket or something – literally beginning to come apart at the seams. Floods of tears, smashing your pots, banging the furniture about. God knows what. Both my wives, God bless them, they've given me a great deal of pleasure over the years but, by God, they've cost me a fortune in fixtures and fittings. All the same. Couldn't do without them, could we? I suppose. Want another one of those?

GEOFFREY   No, thanks.

The door opens. Eva enters

Geoffrey rises and sits again

EVA   (*coming in swiftly and closing the door*) Brrr.

RONALD   Ah.

EVA   Forgot to put my coat on. (*She puts her coat on*)

RONALD   Anything serious?

EVA   No. (*Kneeling by the stove to warm herself*) She says she wants to come down.

RONALD   Here? Is that wise?

EVA   She says she wants a Christmas drink with us since we're all here.

RONALD   Oh well. Sort of thing she does. Calls you all the way upstairs to tell you she's coming all the way downstairs. Your drink there.

EVA   Thanks.

RONALD   And how's that mad dog of yours? Still chewing up your guests?

GEOFFREY   Er – no . . .

EVA   No, we had to – give him away.

RONALD   No, really?

EVA   Yes – he got a bit much. He was really getting so expensive to keep. And then these people we know who've got a farm – they said they'd have him.

RONALD   Oh, dear. I didn't know that. That's a shame.

EVA   Yes, it was an awful decision to make. We just felt – well . . .

GEOFFREY   You did, you mean.

EVA   Darling, we couldn't afford to keep him.

RONALD   Well, old Dick Potter will be relieved, anyway. What did he have to have? Three stitches or something, wasn't it?

EVA   Something like that.

RONALD   Doesn't seem to have done him any harm, anyway. He should be half-way up some Swiss mountain by now. Hopefully, those two lads of ours are safely roped to him.

EVA Oh, is that where they've gone?

RONALD Yes. Something I always meant to take them on myself. Anyway, we'll have to do without old Dick to jolly us up this year. I suppose.

GEOFFREY That's a pity.

The door opens. Marion sweeps in. She wears a negligée. She stands dramatically and flings out her arms

MARION Geoff, darling, it's sweet of you and Eva to come round and see me.

GEOFFREY (*rising*) Oh, that's O.K.

MARION No, you don't know how much it means to me. It really is terribly, terribly sweet of you.

GEOFFREY That's all right, we were . . .

MARION And at Christmas, particularly. Bless you for remembering Christmas. (*She collapses into the armchair*)

RONALD Look, Marion, you're going to freeze to death. For goodness' sake, put something on, woman.

MARION I'm all right.

RONALD Let me get you your coat. You've only just got out of bed.

MARION Darling, I am quite all right. And I am not sitting in my kitchen in a coat. Nobody sits in a kitchen in a coat. Except tradesmen. It's unheard of. Now, offer me a drink.

RONALD Look, dear, you know the doctor said very plainly . . .

MARION (*snapping fiercely*) Oh, for the love of God, Ronnie, it's Christmas. Don't be such an utter misery. (*To the others*) He's Scrooge, you know. He's Scrooge in person. Have you noticed, he's turned all the heating off.

Ronald, dignified, goes to the trolley and pours Marion a drink. Geoffrey sits by the table

Oh, it's heavenly to be up. When you've lain in bed for any length of time, on your own, no-one to talk to, with just your thoughts, don't you find your whole world just begins to crowd in on you? Till it becomes almost unbearable. You just lie there thinking, oh God, it could've been so much better if only I'd had the sense to do so and so – you finish up lying there utterly filled with self-loathing.

EVA I know the feeling.

RONALD (*handing Marion a glass*) Here you are, dear.

MARION Heavens! I can hardly see it. Is there anything in here? No it's all right. I'll just sit here and inhale it. (*Turning to Geoffrey and Eva*) How are you, anyway?

EVA Well, as I told you we're – pretty well . . .

MARION I don't know what it is about Christmas but – I know it's supposed to be a festive thing and we're all supposed to be enjoying ourselves – I just find myself remembering all the dreadful things – the dreadful things I've said – the dreadful things I've done and all those awful hurtful things I didn't mean – oh God, I didn't mean them. Forgive me, I didn't mean them. (*She starts to cry*)

RONALD Look, darling, do try and jolly up just for a bit, for heaven's sake.

MARION (*savagely*) Jolly up? How the hell can – I – jolly – up?

EVA Marion, dear . . .

MARION Do you know what I saw in the hall just now? In the mirror. My face. My God, I saw my face. It was like seeing my face for the first time.

RONALD Oh, come on. It's not a bad face, old sausage.

MARION How could anything be so cruel? How could anything be so unutterably cruel?

RONALD (*to Geoffrey*) Now, you see, this is a case in point. What am I supposed to do? I mean, something I've said has obviously upset her, but you tell me – you tell me.

MARION (*pulling Geoffrey to her*) Geoff – Geoff – Geoff – did you know, Geoff, I used to be a very beautiful woman? I was a very, very beautiful woman. People used to stare at me in the street and say, 'My God, what a beautiful, beautiful woman she is.' People used to come from miles and miles just to take my picture . . .

RONALD Marion.

MARION I mean, who'd want my photograph now? Do you want my photograph now? No, of course you don't. Nobody wants my photograph now. Can anybody think of anyone who'd want a photograph of me now? Please, someone. Someone, please want my photograph.

RONALD (*bellowing*) *Marion!* Nobody wants your damn picture, now shut up.

A silence. Geoffrey and Eva are stunned. Ronald removes his eyeshade and adjusts his scarf

(*The first to recover*) Now then, what were we saying?

The doorbell rings

EVA (*after a pause*) Doorbell.

RONALD Bit late for a doorbell, isn't it?

They sit. The doorbell rings again

EVA Shall I see who it is?

RONALD Yes, do. Have a look through the little glass window. If you don't like the look of them, don't open the door.

EVA Right.

Eva goes into the hall

RONALD Can't think who'd be ringing doorbells at this time of night.

GEOFFREY Carol singers?

RONALD Not at this time. Anyway, we don't get many of them. Marion always asks them in. Insists on filling them up with hot soup and chocolate biscuits as if they were all starving. Had a great row with the chap next door. She made his children as sick as pigs.

Eva enters. As she does so the doorbell rings. She closes the door behind her

79

EVA   I couldn't be sure but it looks suspiciously like the Hopcrofts. Do you want them in?

RONALD   Oh, good grief, hardly.

GEOFFREY   Heaven forbid.

RONALD   If we sit quiet, they'll go away.

EVA   Well, there's the hall light.

RONALD   That doesn't mean anything. People always leave their hall lights on for burglars. I don't know why they bother. I mean, there must be very few households who actually choose to spend their evenings sitting in the hall with the rest of the house in the darkness.

GEOFFREY   If I know the Hopcrofts, they won't give up easily. They'll come round the side.

MARION   Why don't you just go in the hall and shout 'Go away' through the letter-box?

RONALD   Because he happens to have a very large deposit account with my bank.

The doorbell rings

EVA   They can smell us.

RONALD   I think we'll compromise and turn off the lights in here. Just to be on the safe side. (*Going to the door*) Everybody sit down and sit tight. (*By the switch*) Ready? Here we go.

The room plunges into darkness. Just two streams of light – one from the door and one from the window

Now if we all keep absolutely quiet, there's no chance of them – ow! (*He cannons into Eva who gives a cry*) I'm terribly sorry. I do beg your pardon. Was that your . . .?

EVA   That's all right.

GEOFFREY   Ssh.

RONALD   I wish I knew where I was.

GEOFFREY   Well, stand still. I think someone's coming round the side.

EVA   Ssh.

Marion starts to giggle

RONALD Marion. Quiet.

MARION I'm sorry, I've just seen the funny side . . .

GEOFFREY Ssh.

Sidney and Jane appear at the back door. They wear party hats, are decked with the odd streamer, have had more drinks than they are used to and have a carrier bag full of goodies. They both press their faces against the back door, straining to see in

MARION It's them.

GEOFFREY Ssh.

Pause

RONALD I say . . .

EVA What?

RONALD I've got a nasty feeling I didn't lock the back door.

MARION Oh, no . . .

Geoffrey and Eva hide in front of the table. Ronald steps up into a corner by the window. The back door opens slowly

SIDNEY Hallo?

JANE *(unwilling to enter)* Sidney . . .

SIDNEY Come on.

JANE But there's nobody . . .

SIDNEY The door was open, wasn't it? Of course there's somebody. They're probably upstairs.

JANE But, Sidney, they might . . .

SIDNEY Look, would you kindly not argue with me any more tonight, Jane. I haven't yet forgiven you for that business at the party. How did you manage to drop a whole plate of trifle?

JANE I didn't clean it up, Sidney, I didn't clean it up.

SIDNEY No. You just stood there with the mess at your feet. For all the world to see.

JANE Well, what . . .

81

SIDNEY   I have told you before. If you drop something like that at a stand-up party, you move away and keep moving. Now come along.

JANE   I can't see.

SIDNEY   Then wait there and I'll find the light.

A pause. Sidney crosses the room. Geoffrey and Eva creep to the side-board. The light goes on. Sidney and Jane are by the separate doors. The other four are in various absurd frozen postures obviously caught in the act of trying to find a hiding-place. Jane gives a short squeak of alarm. A long pause

MARION   (*eventually*) Boo.

SIDNEY   Good gracious.

RONALD   (*as if seeing them for the first time*) Ah, hallo there. It's you.

SIDNEY   Well, you had us fooled. They had us fooled there, didn't they?

JANE   Yes, they had us fooled.

SIDNEY   Playing a game on us, weren't you?

ALL   Yes.

EVA   Yes, we were playing a game.

SIDNEY   Completely fooled. Walked straight into that. Well, Happy Christmas, all.

ALL   (*lamely, variously*) Happy Christmas.

SIDNEY   (*after a pause*) Well.

JANE   Well.

A pause

RONALD   Would you like a drink? Now you're here.

SIDNEY   Oh, thank you.

JANE   Thank you very much.

SIDNEY   Since we're here.

RONALD   Well. What'll it be? (*He goes to the trolley*)

SIDNEY   Sherry, please.

JANE   Yes, a sherry.

SIDNEY   Yes. We'd better stick to sherry.

82

RONALD   Sherry . . . (*He starts to pour*)

SIDNEY   Sorry if we surprised you.

MARION   Quite all right.

SIDNEY   We knew you were here.

RONALD   How?

SIDNEY   We saw the car.

JANE   Saw your car.

RONALD   Oh. Yes.

A pause. Sidney blows a party 'blower'

EVA   Been to a party?

SIDNEY   Yes.

JANE   Yes.

GEOFFREY   You look as if you have.

SIDNEY   Yes. Up at Walter's place. Walter Harrison.

RONALD   Oh – old Harrison's.

SIDNEY   Oh of course, you'll know him, won't you?

RONALD   Oh, yes.

GEOFFREY   Yes.

SIDNEY   (*to Geoffrey*) Oh, yes of course. Asking you if you know old Harrison. I should think you do know old Harrison. He certainly remembers you. In fact he was saying this evening . . .

RONALD   Two sherries.

SIDNEY   Oh, thank you.

JANE   Thank you very much.

SIDNEY   Compliments of the season.

JANE   Of the season.

RONALD   Yes. Indeed.

A pause

SIDNEY   What a house. Beautiful.

MARION   Oh, do you like it? Thank you.

SIDNEY   No. Old Harrison's. What a place.

JANE   Lovely.

RONALD   Didn't know you knew him.

SIDNEY   Well, I won't pretend. The reason we went was half pleasure and half – well, 'nuff said. Follow me? You scratch my back, I'll scratch yours.

RONALD   Ah.

A pause

JANE   It's a nice kitchen . . .

MARION   At the Harrisons'?

JANE   No. Here.

MARION   Oh. Glad you approve.

A pause

JANE   (*very, very quietly*) Sidney.

SIDNEY   Eh?

JANE   (*mouthing and gesticulating towards the carrier bag*) Their presents.

SIDNEY   What's that? (*He looks at his flies*)

JANE   (*still mouthing and miming*) Shall we give them their presents now?

SIDNEY   Yes, yes, of course. That's why we've brought them.

JANE   We brought you a present.

SIDNEY   Just a little seasonal something.

RONALD   Oh.

MARION   Ah.

EVA   Thank you.

JANE   (*to Eva*) No, I'm afraid we didn't bring you and your husband anything. We didn't know you'd be here, you see.

SIDNEY   Sorry about that.

EVA   Oh, never mind.

GEOFFREY   Not to worry.

JANE   We could give them the hm-mm. You know that we got given this evening.

SIDNEY   The what?

JANE   You know, the hm-mm. That we got in the thing.

SIDNEY   What, that? They don't want that.

JANE   No, I meant for hm-mm, you know. Hm-mm.

84

SIDNEY Well, if you want to. Now, come on. Give Ron and Marion their presents. They're dying to open them.

RONALD Rather.

MARION Thrilling.

JANE (*delving into her carrier and consulting the labels on various parcels*) Now this is for Ron. (*Reading*) To Ron with love from Sidney and Jane.

SIDNEY (*handing Ronald the present*) That's for you.

RONALD Thank you. (*He unwraps it*)

JANE Now then, what's this?

SIDNEY Is that Marion's?

JANE No, that's from you and me to Auntie Gloria. (*Rummaging again*) Here we are. To Marion with love from Sidney and Jane.

SIDNEY This is for you. (*He gives Marion her present*)

MARION Oh, super ... (*To Ronald*) What've you got, darling?

RONALD (*gazing at his present mystified*) Oh, yes. This is very useful. Thank you very much.

MARION What on earth is it?

RONALD Well, it's – er – (*taking a stab at it*) – looks like a very nice set of pipe cleaners.

JANE Oh, no.

SIDNEY No, those aren't pipe cleaners.

RONALD Oh, aren't they?

SIDNEY Good gracious, no.

RONALD Oh, no. Silly of me. Just looked terribly like them for a minute. From a certain angle.

SIDNEY You should know those. It's a set of screwdrivers.

JANE Set of screwdrivers.

SIDNEY Electrical screwdrivers.

JANE You should know those, shouldn't you?

Sidney and Jane laugh. Marion opens her present

MARION (*with a joyous cry*) Oh, look! It's a lovely bottle of gin. Isn't that kind?

RONALD Oh, my God.

SIDNEY   Bit of Christmas spirit.

MARION   Lovely. I'll think of you when I'm drinking it.

JANE   *(still rummaging)* To the boys with love from Sidney and Jane. *(She produces two rather ghastly woolly toys – obviously unsuitable)*

SIDNEY   That's just a little something.

JANE   Just for their stockings in the morning.

MARION   Oh, how nice.

RONALD   They'll love these . . .

SIDNEY   That the lot?

JANE   No, I'm just trying to find the hm-mm.

SIDNEY   Well, it'll be at the bottom somewhere, I should think.

JANE   I've got it. It's nothing very much. We just got it this evening out of a cracker actually. We were going to keep it for our budgie but we thought your George might like it. For his collar. *(She holds up a little bell on a ribbon)*

EVA   Oh.

SIDNEY   So you'll know where he is.

JANE   As if you couldn't guess.

Sidney barks genially and hands them the bell

SIDNEY   Woof woof!

EVA   Thank you.

SIDNEY   *(to Geoffrey)* Woof woof. *(No response)* Woof woof.

GEOFFREY   *(flatly)* Thanks a lot.

SIDNEY   That's your lot. No more.

RONALD   I'm terribly sorry. I'm afraid we haven't got you anything at all. Not really much of ones for present buying.

SIDNEY   Oh, we didn't expect it.

JANE   No, no.

A pause. Sidney puts on a nose mask. Jane laughs. The others look horrified. Marion pours herself a gin

SIDNEY   Well – *(he pauses)* – you know who ought to be here now?

JANE Who?

SIDNEY Dick Potter. He'd start it off.

JANE With a bit of help from Lottie.

SIDNEY True. True.

RONALD Yes, well, for some odd reason we're all feeling a bit low this evening. Don't know why. But we were just all saying how we felt a bit down.

JANE Oh . . .

SIDNEY Oh dear oh dear.

RONALD Just one of those evenings, you know. The point is you'll have to excuse us if we're not our usual cheery selves.

MARION I'm perfectly cheery. I don't know about anybody else.

RONALD That is apart from my wife who is perfectly cheery.

SIDNEY Oh, that's quite understood.

JANE I have those sometimes, don't I?

SIDNEY You certainly do. You can say that again. Well, that's a shame.

RONALD Yes.

EVA (*after a slight pause*) My husband was saying to me just now, Sidney, that he feels terribly guilty that you keep on asking him to do jobs for you and he just hasn't been able to manage them.

SIDNEY Yes. Well, he's a busy man.

EVA Sometimes. But he really is dying to do something for you before long.

GEOFFREY Eh?

EVA He's really longing to.

SIDNEY Oh, well in that case, we'll see.

EVA If you could keep him in mind.

SIDNEY Yes, I'll certainly keep him in mind. Really rather depends.

GEOFFREY Yes, it does rather.

EVA He'd love to.

SIDNEY (*after a pause*) Well now, what shall we do? Anyone

87

got any ideas? We can't all sit round like this, can we? Not on Christmas Eve.

JANE   No, not on Christmas Eve.

SIDNEY   Spot of carpentry, spot of plumbing, eh? I know, what about a spot of electrical work? (*At the radio*) Well, we can have a bit of music to start off with, anyway. (*To Ronald*) This work all right, does it?

RONALD   Yes, yes, but I wouldn't . . .

SIDNEY   Get the party going, bit of music . . . (*He switches on the radio and begins to dance a little*)

JANE   Bit of music'll get it going.

SIDNEY   Hey . . .

JANE   What?

SIDNEY   You know what we ought to do now?

JANE   What?

SIDNEY   We ought to move all the chairs back and clear the floor and . . .

The radio warms up and the room is filled with the sound of an interminable Scottish reel which plays continually. Like most Scottish reels, without a break. This effectively drowns the rest of Sidney and Jane's discussion. He continues to describe with graphic gestures his idea to Jane. Jane claps her hands with excitement. They move the table, stove and chairs out of the way. Sidney then wheels the trolley away past Marion's armchair. She grabs a bottle as it goes by

RONALD   (*yelling above the noise*) What the hell's going on?

SIDNEY   (*yelling back*) You'll see. Just a minute. (*He turns the radio down a little*) Now then. We can't have this. We can't have all these glum faces, not at Christmas time.

JANE   (*scurrying about collecting a bowl of fruit, a spoon, a tea-cosy, colander and tea towel from the dresser and draining-board*) Not at Christmas time. (*She opens the gin bottle and puts a glass near it on the trolley*)

SIDNEY   So we're going to get you all jumping about. Get you cheerful.

RONALD   No, well I don't think we really . . .

SIDNEY No arguments, please.

RONALD Yes, but all the same . . .

SIDNEY Come on then, Eva, up you get.

EVA (*uncertainly*) Well . . .

SIDNEY Come on. Don't you let me down.

EVA No . . . (*She rises*)

GEOFFREY I'm afraid we both have to . . .

EVA No, we don't. We'll play.

GEOFFREY What do you mean, we'll . . .

EVA If he wants to play, we'll play, darling.

Jane begins to roll up the carpet

SIDNEY That's grand. That's marvellous. That's two – come on – any more?

MARION What are we all doing? Is she going to be terribly sweet and wash our floor?

JANE No, we're playing a game.

SIDNEY A game.

MARION Oh, what fun . . .

RONALD Marion, I really don't think we should . . .

MARION Oh, don't be such a misery, Ronnie. Come on.

RONALD Oh . . .

SIDNEY That's telling him, that's telling him. Now then listen very carefully, everyone. This is a version of musical chairs called Musical Dancing.

JANE Musical Forfeits.

SIDNEY Musical Dancing. It's called Musical Dancing.

JANE Oh, I thought it was called Musical Forfeits.

SIDNEY Musical Dancing. It's very simple. All you do – you start dancing round the room and when I stop the music you all have to freeze in the position you were last in . . .

Geoffrey sits on the high stool

Don't let him sit down. (*To Geoffrey*) Come on, get up.

EVA (*sharply*) Get up.

89

Geoffrey gets up

SIDNEY   Only to make it more difficult, the last person caught moving each time gets a forfeit. At the end, the person with the least forfeits gets the prize. (*To Jane*) What's the prize going to be?

JANE   (*producing it from the carrier*) A chocolate Father Christmas.

SIDNEY   A chocolate Father Christmas, right. Everything ready your end?

JANE   I think so.

SIDNEY   Got the list?

JANE   (*waving a scrap of paper*) Yes.

SIDNEY   Right. You take charge of the forfeits. I'll do the music. Ready, everybody? Right. Off we go.

Sidney turns up the music loud. The four stand looking faintly uneasy. Jane and Sidney dance about to demonstrate

Well, come on then. Come on. I don't call that dancing. Everybody dance. Come on, dance about. Keep dancing till the music stops.

Marion starts to dance, in what she imagines to be a classical ballet style. She is extremely shaky

That's it. She's doing it. That's it. Look at her. Everybody do what she's doing. Lovely.

The others begin sheepishly and reluctantly to hop about

And – stop! (*He cuts off the music*) Right. Who was the last?

JANE   Ron.

SIDNEY   Right. It's Ron. Ron has a forfeit. What's the first one?

JANE   (*consulting her list*) Apple under the chin.

SIDNEY   Apple under his chin, right. Put an apple under his chin.

RONALD   Eh? What are you doing?

Jane puts the apple under his chin

JANE   Here. Hold it. Go on, hold it.

RONALD   Oh, don't be so ridiculous, I can't possibly . . .

MARION   Oh, for heaven's sake, darling, do join in. We're all waiting for you. Don't be tedious.

RONALD   (*talking with difficulty*) This is absolutely absurd, I mean how am I to be . . .

SIDNEY   (*over this*) And off we go again. (*He turns up the music*)

They resume dancing. Marion is the only one who moves around: the others jig about on one spot. Sidney shouts encouragement

And – stop! (*He stops the music*)

JANE   Eva!

SIDNEY   Right, Eva. What's Eva got?

JANE   (*consulting list*) Orange between the knees.

SIDNEY   Orange between the knees, right. If you drop it you get another forfeit automatically.

Jane gives Eva her orange

And off we go again.

Music. From now on the forfeits come quick and fast. Jane reading them out, Sidney repeating them. Ronald gets the next (spoon in mouth). The music continues. Geoffrey gets the next (tea-cosy on head). They dance on. Marion gets the next (ironically, swallowing a gin in one). Ronald opens his mouth to protest at this last forfeit of Marion's. In doing so he drops his spoon

(*Gleefully*) Another one for Ron!

JANE   Another one for Ron . . .

RONALD   What?

JANE   Pear on spoon in mouth . . .

SIDNEY   Pear on spoon in mouth . . . (*He gets up on the table and conducts*)

RONALD   Now listen I . . .

Jane rams the spoon handle back in Ronald's mouth. She balances a pear on the other end

SIDNEY   And off we go . . .!

The permutations to this game are endless and Sidney's list covers them all. Under his increasingly strident commands, the dancers whirl faster and faster whilst accumulating bizarre appendages. Jane, the acolyte, darts in and out of the dancers with a dedicated frenzy. Geoffrey throws his tea-cosy to the floor. Jane picks it up and wraps a tea towel round his leg. She then pours another gin for Marion. Sidney, at the finish, has abandoned the idea of stopping the music. He screams at the dancers in mounting exhortation bordering on the hysterical

That's it. Dance. Come on. Dance. Dance. Come on. Dance. Dance. Dance. Keep dancing. Dance . . .

It is on this scene that –

the CURTAIN *falls*

Notes

The notes in this edition are intended to serve the needs of overseas students as well as those of British-born users.

Inverted commas indicate references to stage directions.

An asterisk (*) indicates a colloquial idiom or expression in English.

Absurd Person Singular: for some comments on the play's title, see *Introduction*, pages xxi and xxiii.

Act One

1 '*formica*': type of very hard plastic.

'*dapper*': neat in his appearance.

'*polished hair*': Sidney's hair is plastered down with some kind of oil or lotion that makes it look glossy.

'*Yale knob*': Yale locks, named after a nineteenth-century American inventor, are opened by the simple turning of a knob on the inside of the door, but require a key for their operation on the outside. This fact has an important bearing on what happens later in the scene.

2 * *Cats and dogs*: (raining) very hard.

Eighteen-twenty-three the Hopcrofts' kitchen clock operates on the twenty-four hour system; hence it is now 6.23 pm.

'*fourth wall*': imaginary wall located between the actors and the audience. Sidney (and later Jane) gazes into the audience as if looking at the digital clock mounted on this wall, and reads out the time displayed.

3 '*horn-pipe*': lively dance or jig popular among sailors in pre-steamship days.

5 *killed off my flies*: one of Sidney's feeble jokes, playing on the

double-meaning of 'flies' – the insects and the buttons on a man's trouser front.

6 *'pinny'*: short for 'pinafore'.

11 * *dishy*: beautiful-looking.

12 *plumb it in*: connect up the water supply and the drainage system.

13 *apartheid*: literally, the social system operated in South Africa, under which black and white people are segregated in many areas of life. Here, Marion is merely referring to the fact that, on the washing-machine dial, separate programmes are indicated for white and coloured clothes.
icon: Marion misreads 'iron' as 'icon', a type of religious painting associated most frequently with the Greek Orthodox Church.

15 *knotty pine units*: ready-made panels made of a type of rough-grained pine wood.
the most insistent colour: Marion's thinly disguised way of voicing her disapproval of the lurid colour of the curtains.

16 * *Make our excuses*: Marion is anxious not to have to stay at the party longer than is absolutely necessary. She wants Ronald to tell the Hopcrofts that they have to leave as soon as possible, though without their appearing impolite.
drowned: diluted with so much tonic water that the gin cannot be properly tasted.
I shall . . . morning: as a result of being soaked with the misdirected soda water originally intended for his Scotch.

18 *'wellington boots'*: calf-length waterproof boots, usually made of rubber.

19 *'trilby hat'*: soft felt hat.

20 *'gawps'*: stares, open-mouthed with amazement.

21 *yak*: type of Tibetan ox, noted for its long, silky coat.

22 *The mistletoe's in there*: it is a long standing tradition for sprigs of mistletoe to be hung about the house at Christmas and for people who find themselves together beneath it to give each other a seasonal kiss. Mistletoe is an evergreen parasitic plant that grows on oaks and other trees.

24 *off-licence*: shop licenced to sell alcoholic drinks for consumption off the premises.

26 *general stores*: shop which sells all kinds of foodstuffs and general household supplies.

* *off the cuff*: unofficial.

27 * *striking while the iron is hot*: acting in good time.

* *before it goes off the boil*: before the best time for action passes.

* *it's dog eat dog*: everyone must look after his (or her) own interests.

* *you can scratch mine, I'll scratch yours*: if you look after my interests occasionally, I'll look after yours. The full expression is 'If you scratch my back, I'll scratch yours'.

* *Tit for tat*: you help me and I'll help you.

* *when the chips are down*: at the crucial moment.

* *blow you Jack*: an expression denoting lack of care or concern for the wellbeing of others, usually completed with the words 'I'm all right'.

harem: all the women are crowding round Dick Potter, no doubt admiring his awful jokes.

facets: sides, aspects to his character.

28 *would tickle . . . no end*: would amuse Dick enormously.

29 '*out of his depth*': Sidney feels uncomfortable with the conversation going on between Geoffrey and Ronald.

30 * *cracker*: attractive woman.

P. and O: well-known commercial shipping line.

32 * *on the grapevine*: rumoured.

* *gleam in his eye*: something he anticipates doing with considerable pleasure.

Act Two

36 '*the trendy homespun*': things that are fashionably simple but well-made.

38 * '*nipped in for a quick one*': stopped at a pub for a quick drink.

sexual Flying Dutchman: in the legend, the Dutchman is a ship's captain destined to sail the seas of the world and never find lasting rest or peace. Geoffrey sees his own sex-life as being rather similar.

39 *what I lack . . . ethics*: Geoffrey freely admits that his sexual morality is questionable, but contends that he makes up for this by maintaining high standards of professional conduct – standards reflected in his refusal to work for the despised Hopcroft.

40 * *take a swing at*: hit.

41 '*vertigo*': giddiness brought on by looking down from a high place.

43 '*sticks her head inside*': before the introduction of natural gas for domestic use, many cookers were fuelled by a substance called 'town-gas', a highly toxic by-product of coal. Unfortunately, its poisonous nature made it very popular with people wishing to take their own lives.

peaky: unwell.

44 *Vim*: name of a popular household scouring powder.

45 *No forks. They're Muslims*: many British Muslims are immigrants from countries where it is more usual to pick up food and eat with the fingers than with the forks.

* *Where there's a will*: the complete proverb – 'where there's a will, there's a way' – means that if you want to do something sufficiently strongly, you will find a way of doing it.

* *elbow grease*: vigorous rubbing.

46 * *under the weather*: unwell.

47 * *Brace of shakes*: if you say that you will do something 'in two shakes of a lamb's tail', it means that you intend to do it very soon. 'Brace' is the same as 'two' or 'a pair'.

48 *Where was Moses . . . ?*: reference to the saying 'Where was Moses when the lights went out?'

* *on the go*: busy.

50 * *thingummyjig*: all-purpose word that people use when they cannot remember the proper name for something.

51 *grubs*: small screws.

52 *'tickled'*: amused.

* *a bit – on her pins*: Ronald implies that Marion is a little unsteady on her legs on account of her drinking.

53 *'paint stripper'*: highly corrosive chemical used in the decorating process to remove old paint.

54 *had to give . . . for jumble*: a jumble-sale is one at which money is raised by the sale of items – usually fairly worthless ones – that have been donated for the purpose.

55 *Rabies*: potentially fatal disease transmitted to humans by the bite of an infected animal; associated most closely with mad dogs.

* *groggy*: unwell.

58 * *whajamacallit . . . thingy . . . whosit*: more all-purpose words – see note to *thingummyjig*, page 50 above.

60 * *bits and bobs*: small items of no great importance.

61 * *you-know-whats*: underwear, 'unmentionables'.

62 * *Upsidaisy*: expression used when lifting or helping a child up.

Act Three

66 *'Aga range'*: type of cooking range, usually fuelled by coal or wood, popular in Victorian times and still found today in country houses.

* *on the blink*: out of order.

68 *craving . . . little blue bootees*: pregnant women frequently have cravings (insatiable desires) to eat certain types of food. Ronald is alarmed at Marion's current craving for peanut butter and cheese footballs, thinking that it might indicate that she is expecting a baby. Hence his half-serious enquiry as to whether she is sitting in bed knitting baby clothes.

sedative: drug used to calm people down.

stimulant: substance which causes people to become unusually active.

71 *Trans-Siberian Express*: reference to the freezing conditions in the Brewster-Wrights' house.

   * *knocking them off*: stealing (his drink supply).

73 *unprepossessing*: unimpressive.

74 *bedroom bell*: in larger Victorian houses each room was equipped with an electric bell-push, which connected with a display-board in the kitchen, so that servants could be summoned quickly and easily to any part of the house.

75 * *call it a day*: give up (his marriage).

   * *Under the bridge*: the expression 'it's all water under the bridge' means that there is no reliving the things in our past.

   * *have the hang of it*: know how to cope with something (in this case, marriage).

   * *closed book to me*: something I do not understand.

   to come apart at the seams: all the women in Ronald's life seem to him to have become worn out and disintegrated spiritually, in the way that an old sports jacket does physically.

77 *'negligée'*: woman's light, flimsy dressing-gown.

   Scrooge: a mean-spirited, miserly person, so-called after the central character in Charles Dickens's *A Christmas Carol*.

78 * *old sausage*: a slightly comic term of endearment.

81 *trifle*: dessert made with cake, fruit, custard and cream, often laced with sherry.

83 *'blower'*: party toy consisting of a tightly coiled paper 'tongue' and a mouthpiece. When it is blown, the tongue unwinds and produces a comical noise.

84 *'nuff*: enough.

   * *You scratch . . . yours*: see note to page 27 above.

   hm-mm . . . the thing: Jane is trying to get Sidney to agree to her suggestion of a present for Eva and Geoffrey without anyone else in the room understanding that she is talking about, so adopts a kind of code language.

85 *'taking a stab'*: having a guess.

86 *cracker*: tubular-shaped party novelty made of paper and usually containing a small toy and printed joke or motto.

So called because when it is pulled open a tiny explosive charge is detonated.

budgie: short for 'budgerigar' or Australian parakeet, highly popular as a cage-bird in England.

* *That's your lot*: that's all (there are no more presents).

88 *Scottish reel*: lively Highland dance.

'*tea-cosy*': kind of muffler placed over a tea-pot to keep the tea inside it hot.

90 *forfeit*: penalty.

92 '*strident*': gratingly loud.

'*bizarre*': strange, odd-looking.

'*acolyte*': assistant.

Suggested further reading

If you have enjoyed reading and working on *Absurd Person Singular* you may wish to find out more about Alan Ayckbourn's plays and their creator. Here are some suggestions for further reading:

The plays

How the Other Half Loves, Evans, 1969.
Time and Time Again, French, 1971.
The Norman Conquests, Penguin, 1973. (This is a collection of three independent but related plays: *Table Manners*, *Living Together* and *Round and Round the Garden*.)
Absent Friends, Penguin, 1974.
Bedroom Farce, Penguin, 1975.
Sisterly Feelings, now available as a Longman Study Text, 1979.

The playwright

Ian Watson, *Conversations with Alan Ayckbourn* Macdonald but now out of print. A new completely revised edition is to be published by Faber and Faber in 1988.
Michael Billington, *Alan Ayckbourn*, Macmillan Modern Dramatists, 1983.
Sidney Howard White, *Alan Ayckbourn*, Twayne (Boston, USA) 1984.

Coursework assignments and study questions

For further discussion

Now that you have read and perhaps had the good fortune to see a performance of *Absurd Person Singular*, you might find it helpful to discuss (either in groups or as a whole class) some of the following topics:

1 Which moment from each of the three acts (and also from the play as a whole) did you find the most (a) hilarious (b) thought-provoking (c) touching (d) dramatic (e) absurd? (If you have seen *Absurd Person Singular* in performance, you might also like to discuss whether the same moments stood out for you in the theatre as stood out when you read the play.)

2 Do you feel that the play becomes more or less serious as the three Christmases follow each other?

3 For which of the six characters do you feel the greatest sympathy? For which do you feel the least sympathy? Why?

4 Trace the development of each of the characters through the three acts of the play.

5 What do you think are the central issues raised in *Absurd Person Singular*? Are there any topics which you feel should not have been included in a comedy of this kind? Why?

6 Look back at the topics you discussed before reading the play (pages xxix–xxx). How successfully does the play introduce and deal with these topics?

7 Dick and Lottie Potter might be described as a 'running-joke' that is woven into all three acts of the play. What do you understand by this? How does such a joke work? Can you identify any others in *Absurd Person Singular*?

Oral work

1 *Absurd Person Singular* is full of British idioms and colloquial expressions. Many of these are identified and explained in the Notes (see pages 93–99 where they are marked*). Become familiar with some of these expressions and try to incorporate them into your day-to-day conversations at home and about the school.

At the end of a few days of this activity, hold a class discussion about the effect it had on all the people involved.

2 Another language feature of the play is the use that different characters make of catch words or phrases. In Act One, for instance, Sidney makes frequent use of expressions associated with the Navy, and is heard to mutter 'Dear oh dear' on a variety of occasions. Marion, on the other hand, goes about with such superlatives as 'thrilling', 'marvellous', 'dishy' and 'stunning' on her lips, and always seems to be calling her husband, Ronald, 'darling'. Choose *one* character from the play, find out his or her main catch words and try, by introducing them into your everyday speech, to 'become' him or her for a while.

Again, after a few days, have a post-mortem on this activity. Discuss how certain expressions become associated with particular people and the current catch words and phrases that you, your friends and family are using.

Craftwork assignments

1 Create a poster for an imaginary production of *Absurd Person Singular*. In it, include full-length pictures of two or three of

the characters and a piece of dialogue that aptly illustrates the personality of each. Think carefully about how your chosen characters are described in the play – their clothing as well as their physical appearance – and try to make your representation of them as faithful as possible. If you are not confident about your drawing skills, cut coloured illustrations from discarded magazines and paste them on to your poster-sheet. Do not forget to provide the figures with an appropriate background.

Hold a classroom exhibition of your posters and perhaps award a prize to the one you all judge to be the best.

2 Study carefully Alan Ayckbourn's descriptions of the three kitchens in which the different dramas of *Absurd Person Singular* are acted out. Then do some careful research (using old newspapers and magazines, and perhaps asking a friendly estate agent for help) and try to come up with illustrations of the *kind* of kitchens found in the Hopcroft, Jackson and Brewster-Wright homes. Paste your three illustrations on a single sheet of paper and bring it to class for display and discussion.

As an alternative, imagine what the three sitting-rooms might look like and use them as the basis of the exercise.

3 Create a cartoon character called 'George the dog'. Find out from the play as many details of his appearance, his temperament and his attitude to human beings as you can. Practise drawing George from different angles and in different situations. Then work on a cartoon (either a single frame or a strip) in which we see him in one of the incidents mentioned in *Absurd Person Singular* in which he is involved. Be sure also to include at least one of the play's human characters in your cartoon.

4 Make a graph or wall chart on which you plot the psychological changes that occur to the six people we meet in *Absurd Person Singular*. Along the horizontal axis record the passage of time through the three acts of the play, and on

the vertical axis show the psychological 'highs' and 'lows' that each person experiences. Use a different coloured line for each character. When you have completed your chart, hold a class discussion as to what it reveals.

5 Design and produce the front page of the local newspaper in which the catastrophic collapse of the ceiling of the Harrison building is the lead story.

Drama work

1 Improvise action and dialogue for the following scenes which do not actually occur in *Absurd Person Singular*:

(a) During Act One, Dick and Lottie Potter (complete with 'loud, braying laughs') are left alone in the Hopcroft sitting-room while their hosts are having a minor crisis over Jane's shoes in the kitchen. The text on pages 6–9 will give you some further clues as to what the Potters might be saying to each other. Note that Sidney makes intermittent appearances during this scene.

(b) Recreate the scene in Act Two when Sidney and Jane Hopcroft are left in the Jacksons' sitting-room while Geoffrey goes into the kitchen to find a bottle-opener. Remember the sort of people the Hopcrofts are; that the Jackson flat is on the fourth floor and the lift has broken down; and that George the dog is also in the room, which has just been described by Geoffrey himself as a 'very untidy cesspit'. Check over Pages 41–42 for further helpful details.

(c) Midway through Act Three, having rung the Brewster-Wrights' front doorbell and received no reply, Sidney and Jane Hopcroft work their way round the outside of the house to the kitchen door. How much are they aware of what is going on inside the house? Use the text on pages 79–81 to get some ideas.

2 When Ronald and Marion finally get home at the end of Act One, they discuss the Hopcrofts, their house (especially the kitchen) and the party. Improvise their conversation.

3 Imagine that, in the course of Act One, Eva Jackson finds out the identity of the rain-soaked figure in trilby, mac and wellingtons. She confronts Jane alone in the kitchen. Improvise their conversation.

4 Suppose that Sidney has actually proposed to his guests that they play one of the games he has prepared for the Act One party. Decide who is to be involved and how they might feel about his suggestion. Then try playing the game.

5 There are several occasions in *Absurd Person Singular* when characters say things that they do not mean in order to be civil and not hurt the feelings of others. Imagine what might happen in the following circumstances:

(a) Marion finds the occasion to tell Jane exactly what she thinks of the way she has furnished her home;

(b) Geoffrey shows his true feelings when the Hopcrofts arrive shortly after the start of Act Two;

(c) the Brewster-Wrights and Jacksons greet the arrival of Sidney and Jane Hopcroft in Act Three with open hostility.

6 Improvise some of the conversation that takes place at the party which Sidney and Jane attend at Walter Harrison's house, and from which they have just come when we meet them in Act Three.

7 In groups, choose a self-contained section of the play and work on either a reading or a staging to be performed for the benefit of the rest of your class. After all the performances have been given, discuss whether a reading of this play can work as successfully as a staging. What special considerations does each require of the performers?

Writing assignments

1 Imagine any one of the play's principal characters as a child. What kind of background does he or she come from? Does he/she already possess any of the characteristics or mannerisms that we know him/her to have as an adult? What are his/her chief interests in life? Is there any indication of what kind of work he/she will do when he/she grows up? Write a story about your chosen character as a child.

2 Imagine that Sidney and Jane Hopcropt were childhood sweethearts. Write a story about them in which we see early signs of the relationship they share as grown-ups in the play.

3 Take one of the exercises on which you have been engaged from the 'Drama-work' section above and use it as the basis for a piece of polished writing. Before you start writing, be sure that you have considered carefully (a) the situation, (b) the relationship between the characters involved, (c) their dialogue, and (d) the kind of language in which they usually express themselves. Your writing may take the form of either a short story or a play script.

4 Write two or three successive entries from the diary of any one of the play's characters. Before you start working on this assignment, decide (a) which of the three Christmases the entries refer to, (b) which events from the play should be mentioned, (c) what other events or observations might be included, and (d) what kind of diary the character in question is likely to keep – one that is romantically sentimental, for instance, or one that deals in strict facts, or even one that reveals personal secrets.

5 Write a biographical sketch of Eva as you see her in the course of the play. Next write a sketch of her as Geoffrey sees her. Then write one as Jane sees her. And finally write one as Ronald sees her. How do your different versions

compare? Discuss your sketches with those made by other members of the class.

Try a similar exercise, writing sketches of Sidney as seen by (a) you; (b) Jane; (c) Eva; (d) Marion.

To conclude, write sketches of Ronald as seen by (a) you; (b) Sidney; (c) Marion; (d) Eva.

6 Write the opening pages of your own Act Four of *Absurd Person Singular*, which takes place one Christmas further into the future. Keep to the same six characters with whom we have become familiar and set the scene in one of the kitchens we have already visited in the course of the play. Which is it to be? What developments are likely to have taken place since Act Three? How will you reflect these in your writing? Do not hesitate to include some of Ayckbourn's well-established themes and running-jokes.

7 Twenty years after the events described in the play, Sidney Hopcroft, self-made millionaire, publishes his memoirs entitled *How I got where I am today*. Write Sidney's account of the three years (those covered by the play) in which he began to get established.

Study questions

1 'Don't laugh: it could happen to you.' How real do the moral issues raised in *Absurd Person Singular* appear to you?

2 Are the problems introduced in *Absurd Person Singular* ever satisfactorily resolved?

3 'Beware,' writes Alan Ayckbourn in his personal essay at the beginning of this edition, 'the kingdom of the Hopcroft is at hand.' How gloomy a view of society do you think this is?

4 Why do you think Ayckbourn set his play on three succeeding Christmases?

5 When *Absurd Person Singular* was first staged in the United States, the producer toyed with the idea of reversing the order of the second and third acts, but Ayckbourn insisted on things being left as he had written them. Why do you suppose the two men took the positions they did? Whose side would you be on if the debate were to be reopened?

6 One critic has suggested that the three acts of *Absurd Person Singular* could well be presented as separate, unrelated one-act plays. What, in your view, would be gained or lost if this were to be done?